Praise for RECRUIT!

I have on my desk the original version of this book by Sherle Adams in 1987. I give you my word, this book changed my life and many others, for it was my personal reference and guide on my amazing 25 year journey in direct sales. The fusion of Ro's wisdom with the original is brilliant. Too often we underestimate the power of kindness...a kind word, a compliment, a smile, a sincere and authentic connection in sharing an opportunity that literally could change a life. For contemporary solutions to manifest an abundant, sustainable business in the 'relationship industry', embrace the wisdom of RECRUIT. Your destiny awaits...

~ **Mikki Lessard,** Founder, With Gratitude and Grace

RECRUIT! Brings the wisdom of the ages into the 21st Century and provides secrets of sharing. 'ThinkAbouts' inspire our hearts and 'Activators' get us to make small actions that can create amazing results in your business. RECRUIT! is a must read for anyone wanting to increasing their Sharing Factor!

~ **Tom Judson,** VP Sales Worldwide, Park Lane Jewelry

Ro Shales and G. Sherle Adams have created a clear, easy to read guide on Why and How plus the Benefits of "Connecting with People." This book has excellent self study and group training tools that walk you through the plethora of options to find what works best for you. Even veterans like myself will find pearls of wisdom and expert advice. Be grateful, share this amazing opportunity and enjoy the journey!

~ **Elizabeth Anthony Gronert**, Founding Director, Private Quarters

RECRUIT! This book gives you time tested basics and step by step principles to reach others to make a difference in their life and yours. I've enjoyed the incredible Direct Sales opportunity for 36 years and this book will help you build team strength quickly.

~ **Bonnie Strigenz,** District Director, Jafra Cosmetics International

This book captures the true essence of recruiting. "When you help enough people reach their goals, you cannot help but reach your own goals." The book is filled with Timeless Tips that work! When you master recruiting there is no limit for your success in Direct Sales.

~ **Sandi Mullins**, Former VP of Sales, Tupperware Inc. Currently building the sales team at Union Springs Wellness

Roseann and Sherle are powerhouses! If you want to succeed in Direct Sales, you will move ahead faster with this book. You'll enjoy every minute of the wise and sage advice.

~ **Brenda Dahl J.D.**, Dahl Law Offices

RECRUIT! provides sage wisdom of practical and tactical approaches to building business - the smart way. This book is full of purposeful ThinkAbouts and useful Activators for new and tenured business builders who are ready to master the timeless fundamentals of building winning relationships.

~ **Maggie Mongan**, The Business Rescue Coach & President of Brilliant Breakthroughs, Inc.

Success in Direct Selling is all about building an organization. Love of your product and personal sales can only take you so far. Roseann has created an amazingly practical book to help anyone become successful in Direct Selling. It is packed with real world experience and advice that will be invaluable to anyone who reads the book and takes action.

~ **Mark Bosworth**, CEO SwissJust North America

RECRUIT! motivated me to pick up the phone and make calls! It also reminds me of all the great reasons why I love to share the business with everyone, everywhere, and why recruiting & sharing truly offer everyone the greatest reward.

~ **Carol Judson**, Franchise President, Aloette Southeast

This action packed read not only invigorates, it is hands down the best accountability book I have read. RECRUIT! leaves the reader with the knowledge that Action = Results is the name of the game of recruiting, and the key to building an organization others only dream about!

~ **Cindy Juncaj**, President and CEO/ Partner, Demarle at Home

RECRUIT! will become your "go to" source on many levels. It will help you feel good about connecting to others with your opportunity and offer you insight into helping your team to reach out to others. I'm amazed at the volume of activities, ideas and inspiration available. Like me, you'll reach for it again and again!

~ **Julie Mucha**, VP Sales Weekenders USA, retired, Executive Distributor at NuSkin

I appreciate the Universal language in this book. I believe it can be applied to absolutely any organization or corporation. There are many paths, yet there is One Way. RECRUIT! encompasses the One Way.

~ **Reverend Lisa Marie Teubel**

There's nothing like experience to support success in any business venture, and Roseann shares her experience in a bright and clear way in this book. The suggestions are helpful and understandable. Follow them, and you are sure to do well.

~ **Linda San Filippo**, Vollara Distributor - Air/Water Purification Systems

First published in the United States of America
March, 2012 by IC Publishing Group a division of
Imaginative Consulting LLC

RECRUIT!

Connecting with People to Change Your Business and Your Life

Cover Design and Layout by Dorothy Hall

ISBN-13: 978-1-938351-00-6
ISBN-10: 1938351002

Printed in the United States of America

RECRUIT!

Connecting with People to Change Your Business and Your Life

Roseann Shales

Inspired by G. Sherle Maguire Adams

Dedication

I dedicate this book to my husband, Robb Shales, and our sons, Robbie and Ricky, for their endless patience and support as I continue to evolve as a person, wife and mother; to my Dad, George Baldauf, who nurtured my entrepreneurial spirit; my Mom, Sally Baldauf, who taught me to be kind and generous; and to my mentors and all of the strong and wise Baldauf women (both born and married into my extended family), who encouraged me to be big and bold and to persevere.

And especially to my writing partner and long time friend, Sherle Maguire Adams, better known internationally as "Grandma Sherle," who is the original source of the ThinkAbout and Activators concept and style. She is an amazing woman who paved the way for an entire generation of women in advertising and marketing when it really was a man's world. Then she found Direct Sales and her true calling, inspiring hundreds of thousands of people to go after what they want and get it as independent business people. Her list of accomplishments takes pages and pages. She is loving and wise and everyone's perfect Grandma!

Finally, this book is dedicated with great gratitude, to YOU and to the 15.8 million* people in America, plus millions more around the world, who are finding personal independence, more time, financial freedom, and the joys of being an entrepreneur in Direct Sales.

**DSA Annual survey 2010*

Who will benefit from this book?

If you're NEW to the Direct Sales Industry, enjoy sharing and want to succeed, you will learn how to connect to enhance your natural communication skills.

If you're a LEADER or a Team Builder and want to grow your business more quickly, you will relate to sensible new ideas about the mental and emotional barriers that hinder getting a Yes!

If you're a TRAINER who wants to be more effective you'll be delighted with how what you teach will be reinforced with participation-creating Activators ©

If you want to REACH OUT more effectively, you'll get insight into why good caring people can be inhibited from recruiting* others until they understand the barriers that block success.

If you recruit VOLUNTEERS for a non-profit, church work, or political help, make your life easier by learning how to get more people to say Yes!

If you're an ENTREPRENEUR you'll be pleased with the tax advantages, time, and financial freedom that come with the joy of helping people make their dreams come true.

**Recruiting is the universal word we use for Sharing, Sponsoring, Enrolling or Joining.*

If there is a better word than

CONNECTING

we do not know what it is.

Connecting gives joy to you and others
Connecting enriches with more than money
Connecting enhances personal growth
Connecting is what people want to learn
Connecting plus sharing create success
Connecting is what this book is about

Connecting

Read on. Learn why it works.
~ Roseann "Ro" Shales & Grandma Sherle

Contents

Who Will Benefit from this Book? vii
Connecting viii
The Sharing Effect 1
Reasons to Recruit 5
The Process of Recruiting 7
ThinkAbouts and Activators 9
What is Recruiting? 11
What Gets in the Way? 25
Finding Prospects 39
Finding More Prospects 61
Making Connections 73
Developing Relationships 83
Building Your Business 93
Talking to Yourself 111
The Importance of Recruiting Appointments 125
70 Approaches that Work! 130
Dealing with Resistance 139
Grandma Sherle on Communication 141
Appreciate What You Have in Direct Sales 145
So What's Next? 147
"Thanks" to Some Very Special People 151
Ordering, Speaking & Contact Information 152
About the Authors 153

The Sharing Effect

My coauthor, Grandma Sherle Adams, and I have almost 100 years of experience in the Direct Sales Industry. It is our pleasure to connect you to practical ideas and new methods to grow and increase your personal and professional success.

We have served as consultants at many levels, from working in the field as Independent Representatives and Leaders, just like you, to carving careers consulting to CEOs and on Management Teams. We have always remained conscious of your needs in the field.

Our major interest has always been the recruiting process and how important it is to get people started quickly, with a clear focus on early success. Like you, we have supported individuals through personal fears and barriers that blocked their recruiting and business success.

This book is about what we have learned from our own experience and from working with Leaders at all levels.

> **It's about connecting** with people to change your business and your life!
>
> **It's about sharing** the wonderful opportunity that you have as a direct seller to take control of your future with your own business.
>
> **It's about feelings** common to people who recruit others. It's about finding and approaching people and about how people think and feel, or should think and feel, about recruiting.
>
> **It's about what you can do** to make it easier for you and your team to find, recruit and retain new people.
>
> **It's about becoming a force** for good in the world by supporting others and encouraging them to focus on objectives that create a better life and a lifestyle to enjoy as a direct seller.

Whatever your reason for starting your business, realize various things may sometimes get in the way of your success. Fortunately, most are identifiable and *fixable*. In this book you'll find the tools you need to succeed. "ThinkAbouts©" and "Activators©" were developed to increase your understanding and ability to overcome challenges that get in your way.

"ThinkAbouts" are brief, thought-provoking messages relating to feelings and ideas. They'll help you to think about doing the things you want to do in better and simpler ways.

"Activators" offer you and your team innovative actions and activities to reinforce the messages and to stimulate ideas and ways to learn from discussions and self or group analysis.

We know from experience that for most people learning is not an instantaneous process. That's why reading is not enough. Learning is experiential. People learn best by assimilation and utilization. This book helps you do just that.

This book and training tool is meant for everyone with a desire to build a team. You will also find that much of what we share applies at home with family and friends, in the workplace with managers and employers, and in volunteer organizations.

We share ideas to contribute to your growth through more effective recruiting and faster development of your new people. You'll learn how to harness the power of connecting, sharing and caring to naturally retain more of the people you bring in. This helps everyone - you, your recruits, and your company.

We've worked with many Leaders and have found common traits among them, including a caring heart and a desire to share their business opportunity consistently. These traits made those Leaders big winners and big earners in their companies. People succeed by leading the way and showing others how to succeed.

It takes effort to reach out to people and offer a sincere compliment or word of encouragement or, even better, the offer of an opportunity to enhance someone's future. You can be a force for good in the world by speaking up and sharing.

The more successful you become, the more important it is to be a good example for other people. Watch your words and thoughts, they are contagious. Your consistent thoughts become real as you take action and create your own success (or lack of it). Your team will duplicate what you do and say. You are their role model. Be positive, be uplifting, be kind, and always do what you say you will do. My first mentor, Sandi Mullins, taught me; "With every opportunity comes responsibility." As a Leader you are responsible for your team's growth. Your consistent development of people makes a big difference in your company and the world.

We want you to be consistently intrigued with communication, how people talk to each other at all levels. Grandma Sherle says, "No matter what kind of situation we are in, we are only words apart." Our intent is to help you understand this truth. We want you to learn things about communication and self motivation that will apply to your whole life.

Sometimes it's easier to find the words to say than to understand the feelings behind those words. Almost everyone has some emotional barriers or fears they have carried forward from childhood into adulthood. The thoughts, emotions, or feelings of your team and prospects can get in the way of truly hearing what other people say and what they really mean.

We want you to become a richer person by exploring people's feelings as you are becoming a better Leader and recruiter. One of your most important roles is to help your people feel good about who they are and what they offer, so they are able to reach out to others and duplicate what they know.

This book puts a strong focus on feelings and emotions. We want to maximize your good feelings and help you tune into the feelings of your prospects and your team in order to develop the potential in the people who have a real desire to move ahead.

We will inspire you to have more empathy for others and to increase your ability to recognize emotional needs. We want to make your challenges clear and show you logical solutions to conquer those challenges.

I know a psychologist who asks patients to do this exercise for 30 days; look in a mirror every morning and say, "I am a worthwhile person and the world is a better place because I am in it." After 30 days in a row most people begin to believe it. Try it.

The fact that you are reading this book says very specifically that you are worthwhile. You want to know more about how to help yourself and others reach out to share the business that you enjoy and the lifestyle you are creating.

This is not a book to be read once and put on your bookshelf. Instead, it's also a tool to use for years. When you share Think-Abouts and Activators, you'll grow personally, increase the size of your team, and build your income. Understand that effective communication opens many doors to enlarge your life.

This material will be most useful to you when you realize the value and potential power in it. Take in the ideas and information slowly, not in one big gulp.

Our Suggestion is to:

SKIM - to get an idea of what is included.

SCAN - for challenges people might face. Highlight as you read.

STUDY - think about your team, business, and meetings.

SELECT - the first things you want to use, apply and share.

Use the ideas, inspiration and information to serve you in two ways. We give you the ***why*** along with the ***how*** to build relationships and to stay personally motivated. You will discover what fun it is to lead and grow along with your team.

There are many advantages in a Direct Sales Business. You empower personal choice and freedom. You give the gift of options in life for people to choose. Never underestimate the value of choices. There are many people who need what you offer. Some you already know, some you have not met, yet. They are around you every day, everywhere you go. Open your ears and eyes and tune in to people. Be aware, be prepared to share. Be a strong role model. Be proud of your business decision and be loyal to your company.

Start recruiting with the materials, tools, and processes your company provides for you. Use this book as a tool to amplify what you've been given. Create duplication for consistent growth. Your long term business success is based on duplication. It's wise to teach only what others can copy. When you keep it super simple, your team will replicate what you do. Together, you'll build strong teams of successful people.

When you are recruiting, remember the needs and desires of your potential recruit are the most important things. Always have their best interests in mind. You can make a great impact by encouraging others to live up to their potential. The immeasurable contributions you make change lives in remarkable ways.

You know the job you have to do. Ready? Great! Let's get started!

With great joy,

Roseann "Ro" Shales

Reasons to Recruit

This is the best time ever to share your business opportunity! The economy has been in turmoil for several years. People are looking for choices now more than ever before. People in all age groups from the Baby Boomers through the Millennials (that covers 18-66 year olds), people at all educational levels from high school through college and advanced degrees, women and men alike want more choices. They want to learn and to grow and to create their future without depending on someone else.

Consider the number of ads, flyers, TV and radio interviews, magazine articles, e-mails, webinars and messages, about ways to achieve personal growth and self improvement. People are seeking new and better ways to experience personal growth, to have rewarding lives, to have financial security, and the ability to control their destiny. People want to give more, to share more, and even to love more.

Isn't it wonderful there are people like you who can offer for FREE or low cost what people spend thousands of dollars to experience? You are in an industry where everything is built around self-improvement, personal growth and choices. As an informed Direct Seller building your own business, you don't have to spend a lot of money to advertise. Your company does it for you through websites, blogs, webinars, marketing materials, and catalogs.

Even better, you and the people you recruit have almost daily opportunities for personal growth and professional development that are available to you in exchange for your time and a little bit of effort. You receive information, tips, and techniques from all of the successful people around you. You can participate in conference calls and webinars from your company, listen to podcasts on your MP3 player or even attend a meeting or conference virtually. You are rewarded financially by applying what you learn to increase your income.

You're learning to be a better listener and to talk to people in ways that show you really care about them, their wants, needs, and dreams. You can offer them free training, and ways to grow personally and professionally from the day they join you. People go to business school to study how to run a successful business. You don't need to do that. Your company spends money to take care of all the big aspects of business: planning, sourcing product, purchasing, manufacturing, service, and delivery plus a generous compensation plan, all to support your personal and business growth.

You are in the people business and the more people you have on your team, the bigger your business can grow. As your business increases in size, your income increases and your expenses may even decrease depending on your company's incentives. You get, for free or low cost, a valuable and worthwhile education because you took charge of your future and now you choose to support others to do the same.

As you grow your business, each new recruit allows you to leverage your income so the team can be working for you, even when you're not. You have the opportunity to plant seeds and see the incredible crops of money and people growing exponentially. You'll enjoy the satisfaction of being an important influence in the growth of so many people.

Sometimes your personal reason for being in business, your *why*, may not be meaningful enough. It doesn't drive you steadily. Maybe you are seeking something to lead you past whatever barrier is getting in your way to consistent work and real commitment. Adding new recruits focuses your energies. They require you to be in your "A" game, to teach them best practices, and to role model how to succeed.

In any organization some people recruit even though they initially hadn't planned to. Why? They are competitive with others or with themselves. They want more and realize recruiting is the way to get it. They welcome new insights and ideas. There are also the people out there NOT recruiting even if they seriously need the extra income. Doesn't it make sense to take advantage of all of the income available to you by sharing your business opportunity?

Why should you recruit? To share the opportunity that was given to you. To increase your skills, your success, and to grow personally while achieving your highest potential and developing the same attributes in others. Recruiting is the best way to reap all of the rewards of your compensation program, to earn incentives, recognition, and rewards. Keep recruiting to join the ranks of the elite, the top Leaders in your company, and take advantage of the whole career plan.

The Process of Recruiting

You probably have a company system to follow and language to describe each step of doing your business and every specific process (i.e. recruiting, selling, or training.) Always utilize company materials and company language. You want everyone you recruit to talk the business and do the business the same way as you do, so you can duplicate your success.

As you grow, you will discover the power and good sense of duplication. You always want to set an example to discourage people from doing things in their own way or to constantly be trying something new because they are bored with the company way. It literally ends up wasting time and money for everyone.

Regardless of what your company calls the steps in their system, there is a common process. We want you to understand the process because, when you do, it will be easier for you to move ahead. There are three basic steps involved: Exploring – Enrolling - Educating.

STEP 1: Exploring

Connecting, Sourcing, Prospecting, Sharing

This includes anything that has to do with finding, talking to, and developing new prospects including setting a specific date and time for a meeting about what you offer.

STEP 2: Enrolling

Presenting, Demonstrating, Interviewing

This involves all the things you do to share the business story and what you do when you tell it. It includes asking questions to get to know the prospect, sharing your personal story, why someone should work with your company, compensation information, and asking for a decision to join you in business today.

Questions are an important part of a presentation because they help you understand your prospect as you begin to build a relationship, and it takes good questions to get a commitment. Whenever you share your business information, ask for a decision to join right now.

STEP 3: Educating

Training, Developing, Mentoring

The education process begins as soon as you enroll a new recruit and it never stops! To succeed as a Leader, educating yourself and your team must be ongoing.

Initial training or orientation is where basic information is presented so that new team members can successfully start their business. Your recruit's business objectives, their personal reason or ***why*** they joined is discussed and initial goals are set with a plan to achieve them and build a solid business foundation.

It is wise to set up accountability and then structure how you are going to work together in your new business relationship. Treat each recruit according to their goals and dreams and *match their energy and interest level.*

Always keep recruiting. It's the way to count your blessings!

ThinkAbouts and Activators

Maximizing the Benefits

ThinkAbouts

Read them one at a time, thoughtfully considering if it applies to you or anyone you care about. Consider how to use it personally or with a group where it might be used as a springboard to discuss related issues.

Utilize related Activators to reinforce a particular ThinkAbout concept. Doing this will help you get the full emotional impact of reflection and group discussion. Not all ThinkAbouts have an Activator, however, Activators may apply to multiple ThinkAbouts in the same section.

Activators

There are many questions to ask about any ThinkAbout to encourage discussion and sharing of ideas and challenges.

Here are a few thought starters:

- What does this mean to you?
- Does your reaction remind you of something you should do?
- Does this remind you of anyone you know?
- Can you think of anything to talk about that relates in any way to this particular ThinkAbout?
- What kind of activity could you plan on this subject for future learning or training?
- Would additional training on this subject be helpful?
- If you had to plan a meeting or give a talk on this subject what might you mention that we did not?
- Is there anything you should personally practice to increase your results?

We invite your comments!

We would love to hear from you regarding your thoughts and experiences with ThinkAbouts, Activators, and all the other ideas in RECRUIT!

Log on to the website and take the short book survey.

www.imaginativeconsulting.com/recruitsurvey

Share your favorites. Share how the ThinkAbouts and Activators have helped you and your team to grow. Share what you like best. Let us know if there is anything you didn't like.

Share your suggestions and requests for new topics and sections. If we use your suggestion we will acknowledge you for it in the next edition.

We are grateful for you!

1 - 8

What is Recruiting?

Recruiting is sharing 12
Recruiting is helping 14
Recruiting is growing 16
Recruiting is stretching 18
Recruiting is planning 20
Recruiting is giving 22
Think of the joy in sharing 23
It's a privilege to recruit 24

Recruiting is sharing

Once you recognize the essence of sharing, something you might see as a task or something you ought to do more becomes something you want to do more.

Take a moment to think about what you are actually doing when you are recruiting.

You share good feelings about your business. You share the fact that your opportunity is open to others.

When you recruit, you offer hope and a way to earn extra money to those who may love their job but not the size of their paycheck.

You share a way to "job-test" a rewarding new career for the many employed people who hate their jobs but like what they perceive as security.

Recruiting is a logical and wonderful way to teach that real security comes from independence.

Activator 1

TALK ABOUT

How would you define what security means to you? What do you feel security means to most people? How secure is the average employee? And how does being a successful independent contractor help contribute to your feeling of security?

What goes through your mind when you help people have better feelings about their security?

Can you think of any reasons for not sharing good news about having security as a result of being independent? Does everyone on your team (including your Leader or coach) agree these reasons are valid? If not, why not?

SELF-ANALYSIS

If you were asked to describe the feelings you have when you do something nice for someone, what would you say? How would you feel if you had the opportunity to share something helpful, and you didn't do it because you were too lazy, busy, unmotivated or afraid?

PEER OR GROUP DISCUSSION

DISCUSS how much sharing goes on in your business and how it affects personal and team success.

ASK how the concept of sharing relates to recruiting and explore the benefits.

Recruiting is helping

There are people who are bored, who need money, who feel unappreciated.

There are people who see no future in their company and don't know if or when they will get a raise in pay.

There are people who dream about being their own boss and then have no idea of how to make their dream come true. And that's exactly what you can do!

Part time or full time, you can offer a method and hope. And, in a very practical way, you can help these people begin building independent businesses and take control.

You'll show them how to be happy building a business with their choice of flexible hours to have real time freedom.

They'll decide how much they want to earn, knowing they can do it with your help and their commitment.

Why in the world would you ever decide not to offer this and deny yourself the joy of helping?

Activator 2

WRITE

Make a list of the kind of life situations you are glad you are not in. Consider people who have financial or emotional problems such as being broke, feeling lonely, or knowing they are not fully utilized or appreciated. Put a check mark by the situations on your list that could be changed by working in a business like yours.

SELF-ANALYSIS

Did you find it difficult to make this list? Are you aware of other people enough to sense their problems? Did you hesitate about deciding your kind of work, new friends, and new activities could be considered a solution? Is it possible that because your life is on a better track, you find it hard to relate to them what you have to offer? Ask yourself why.

ROLE-PLAY

Pick out someone to pretend to be a widow, newly divorced, a retiree, a need-extra-money executive, a young mother (or father), an empty nester, a newlywed, a teacher with the summer off, or a successful professional unhappy in their job. Now try to recruit that person. Later share your feelings as the recruiter and ask the prospect to share their feelings too. Talk about what you learned and what you, as the recruiter, could do differently. Have everyone who is observing share their ideas.

PEER/GROUP DISCUSSION

CREATE a list of life situations that might create interest in your opportunity: planning a wedding, starting a family, buying a house, saving for college, retirement, empty nest, unemployed or underemployed, downsized, successful but discontented, or just a desire for a better future. **DISCUSS** which approaches to use for each situation and innovative ways to meet potential recruits.

Think About 3

Recruiting is growing

Forget about the money or the recognition and the rewards of building your own organization or team.

Just for a moment forget the tangibles that come your way when you become a successful recruiter.

Think instead of the many personal growth intangibles.

Include the blossoming you'll frequently see in the people you bring into the business.

For some reason nature did not intend for anything to grow alone. That's why there are ever-seeding winds.

When you recruit, you grow in your ability to spread the word and understand enough to reach out to help others.

You grow in your ability to encourage, teach, and support as you develop your skill for mentoring others.

You plant seeds that without your help might have been lost or blown away and wasted.

Activator 3

WRITE

Make a list of the ways that recruiting can help you grow. Consider the financial, intellectual, emotional, and psychological aspects. Also make a detailed list of how your recruiting someone might contribute to their growth.

SELF-ANALYSIS

Now check the lists. Put an X after every way that you have grown to the maximum (if you believe that's possible). Then put a check mark next to the ways you'd like to feel you're still growing. If you have no check marks ask yourself why.

DRAW

You don't have to be an artist to draw this visual. Start by drawing a big clay pot. This is your life. Pretend the pot is full of soil and seeds. Draw a tall stem to show several inches above the edge of the top. The stem is your business. Now put a flower at the top of the stem. This is your success. Next draw some leaves. These are your customers, friends and associates. If you've already recruited people insert some stems to represent your recruits. And if they've already recruited, add flowers on each. Now draw a dotted line stem for all the recruits you will add. Smile! You are now sharing and planning to share more, and as a result will earn wonderful rewards, both tangible and intangible.

PEER OR GROUP DISCUSSION

Use the clay pot visual as the focus for a discussion on how to nourish growth. **ASK:** What are you going to do to assure these stems are rooted (trained)? What are you going to do to assure they'll bloom (get started)? What are you going to do to encourage them to reproduce (recruit)? And how do you intend to turn dotted lines into more stems (new recruits)?

Recruiting is stretching

What if we exercised just enough to not affect our comfort level?

What if we set goals so easy to achieve that we hardly had to try?

What if we never reach out for more than we can see, how would we ever avoid boredom and stagnation?

Wouldn't we become *sleeping settlers* (Couch Potatoes) instead of being *daring dreamers* (Entrepreneurs)?

Recruiting stretches and strengthens our motivation to reach out. It provides a way to exercise our ability and our willingness to help others to stretch their natural skills (and often unrecognized ability) to turn their dreams into their reality.

They say when you are physically exhausted, exercising will give you renewed energy. It is the same thing when you get up and exercise your recruiting muscles. Try it!

Activator 4

TALK ABOUT

What do recruiting and exercise have in common? To be a good recruiter, you need to be dedicated to developing certain muscles. Let's call these muscles: prospecting, approaching, convincing, committing, and supporting. Which ***muscle*** do you need to work on most? Why? How can you strengthen that muscle?

WRITE

Having picked a ***muscle*** that needs developing, write out an objective and a plan for achieving that objective. Think about this as an exercise program to improve your recruiting strengths.

SELF-ANALYSIS

To exercise regularly takes motivation. What's your motivation for exercising and toning up your recruiting muscles? If you are not highly motivated, can you think of something you really want that recruiting will help you get? And what can you do to get it sooner than you ever imagined?

ASK YOURSELF SOME QUESTIONS:

Am I in business for fun or just part-time income? Or am I building the foundation for a career and considerable income whenever I want it?

PEER OR GROUP MEETING

ASK: if any of the recruiting muscles (prospecting, approaching, convincing, committing and supporting) are underdeveloped? How are you handicapped in terms of getting long-term results?

DISCUSS: What do you feel are your weakest and strongest recruiting muscles?

ASSIGN: Specific ***muscle-building*** exercises or goals for a specified period of time. Schedule a follow up time.

Think About 5

Recruiting is planning

Financial planning is a major aspect of building a successful business. Planning to recruit adds to your income and prevents leaving any money lying on the table if you don't share what you have to offer.

Add to the emotional reasons to recruit, the plain, simple fact that you will not make extra money if you do not recruit.

When you plan to build and work with your team, you are leveraging your time.

When you are a recruiter you will have people out there doing what you trained them to do and making money for themselves as they make money for you.

That's what planning and leveraging is all about.

When you make what you do duplicatible, you will see steadily increasing amounts on your paycheck. So stick to your company system. Don't try to *reinvent the wheel.*

Get multiple benefits. As you recruit, your paycheck grows, you will get promoted and you will develop Leadership skills.

As a side effect, you'll become a better planner in all areas of life.

Activator 5

WRITE

Use the pro/con technique. Entitle a sheet of paper with this question, "Do I want to be an effective recruiter?" Then draw a vertical line down the center and put Pro on one side and Con on the other. Now list every single thing you can think of that is positive and negative about recruiting. Consider every aspect of recruiting: emotional, psychological, and financial.

SELF-ANALYSIS

Before you do anything else, find a quiet place and go over and over this list. Use this list to try to analyze where your head really is when it comes to planning in order to recruit consistently.

TALK ABOUT

What might you have to give up to find more time to look for and talk to potential recruits? Is it watching a TV show? Or a hobby? Cutting back on tennis or golf? Or meeting with friends for wine or shopping? Or going to the movies? Is it possible that you don't have to give up anything? Maybe you just have to organize your time better. Think about what you could do if you spent thirty minutes a day approaching potential recruits.

PEER OR GROUP DISCUSSION

Compare lists. Do they include *helping someone* versus *denying someone*? Or *willing to hear a no* versus *can't stand hearing no*? What did others have on their list that you missed? Now share some time-saving ideas about how you can find more time to build your business.

Think About 6

Recruiting is giving

If you sum it all up, recruiting is something very special because recruiting is giving.

You give to yourself and to others when you make the time to recruit consistently. Someone gave this opportunity to you and you pass it on.

You are generous and care about helping others find the joy, fulfillment, and rewards that you enjoy.

Recruiting is helping, growing, stretching, sharing and planning. You are serious about building your income through giving others what you enjoy and benefit from.

You recruit because you consider your own business an important aspect of your life.

You recruit because you are smart and take the time and make the effort to build your future.

You recruit because you like reaching out to help people.

When you give more, you receive more in return, in all areas of your life.

Think of the joy in sharing

When you are recruiting, aren't you actually doing a happy thing by sharing good news?

Think about the tough things people think about, worry about, and get frustrated about every day.

Imagine all the people out there who are feeling that they don't have any options. Then think about the options that you can offer.

If you could be of help, would you, could you decide not to do something? Could you walk away when someone needs what you have to share?

If there were a way to give people an option and hope for a brighter future, could you imagine not sharing and offering an opportunity for change?

Or would you thank the powers that be you have something to share to enhance lives and realize you do well in your business by doing good for others?

Choose to share your opportunity every day and bring joy into the lives of the people you meet. Just do it.

It's a privilege to recruit

Being effective is not just a result of professionalism or learned or practiced skills.

Being an effective recruiter is similar to being a good friend, caring sibling or loving parent.

You have hundreds, even thousands of skills that are so natural you never even think about them.

Many of these skills are exactly what will make you a sincere and successful recruiter.

If you care, if you want to help others, if you are willing to reach out to people, to sometimes get a "no" and to keep on going, you will succeed.

Recruiting is simple and effective if you think of your opportunity as a gift to give to someone.

Consider yourself among the privileged that are in a position to make a difference in the lives of others.

9 - 17

What Gets in the Way

Why some people don't recruit 26
You say you're embarrassed............................ 28
Not everyone likes selling 30
Is the whole picture too big?........................... 32
Watch out for the rocks!.................................. 34
Enthusiasm can be a disadvantage 35
Examine your feelings...................................... 36
What are you responsible for? 37
Always keep recruiting.................................... 38

Think About 9

Why some people don't recruit

You will often hear non-recruiters give the excuse they aren't comfortable doing what they have actually been doing most of their life.

So explore what is causing their discomfort in this kind of situation. After all, they have recommended things before, so why not recommend an opportunity?

Is it because they may receive personal benefits they may feel they don't deserve?

Is it because they don't realize the compliment inherent in the selection of someone to whom they are going to offer the opportunity to improve their life?

Is it selfishness, because their ego is so strong they feel better qualified to do this business than someone else might be?

Or is it that they're simply making an excuse about doing something they don't yet feel they know how to do? And, if you recruited them, what is your excuse for not making them feel more comfortable?

Activator 9

WRITE

Make a list of every excuse you have ever heard from someone who is not recruiting or not doing an effective or consistent job of recruiting.

ROLE-PLAY

If you aren't a trainer, pretend you are. Take each excuse on the list and team up with someone and role-play how you would handle it. After the role-play is completed take turns and talk about your feelings or reactions, and what you might say to be more effective.

SELF-EVALUATION

Ask yourself whether some of the responses you gave as *trainer* surprised you? Why? Do some of the answers make sense to you in terms of your current recruiting behavior and results?

SELF-MOTIVATION

What can you do to motivate yourself to recruit more consistently and to improve and practice recruiting skills? Consider new goals, new reasons, new ways to keep score or compete or a specific recruiting commitment to someone other than yourself.

PEER AND GROUP DISCUSSION

PLAY the game "Recruiting Excuses." One Person gives a serious or funny excuse. The second person answers it. The third person scores the answer. Score is based on 0 -10 with 10 being really good. Then rotate and repeat the process. Discuss what happened. **ASK** if there is anyone who is willing to admit that they have been using a particular excuse and they are resolved to give it up. How will you follow up?

Think About 10

You say you're embarrassed

That's why you never talk about your business or opportunity in social situations. You don't want your friends to think you are there to sell them something.

Well, consider this: how do you respond when people ask you what you've been doing lately? Or ask if you are still at the same job? Or talk about how well or happy you look?

What do you say when someone wishes they could go on a trip and you have just returned from where they want to go? Or you traveled somewhere glamorous because with your extra income you can afford it.

Or what do you say when someone expresses a worry, or a wish, or maybe a desire to do something, and you know that what you have to offer might help?

Isn't it okay to say; "Thanks for sharing that, it gives me an idea. I'm going to call you this week!"

Then you can save your recruiting talk for a future time and go right on with your socializing.

Activator 10

TALK ABOUT

How many people do you know socially who are working but don't like their job or are frustrated or discontent? What percent of the people you know, or may meet socially, might consider joining you if they could be open to putting the focus on giving service rather than on selling?

SELF-ANALYSIS

Assuming you like the people you meet at social, community or church events, don't you feel that those who might be even a little bit interested are entitled to know about the opportunities offered by your company? If you don't feel that way, you should do some self-examination and try to discover why.

ROLE-PLAY

Make up some social situation, role-play comments and questions that you might hear in a social situation that could be considered as an opportunity for a curiosity-creating approach. In your role-playing observe whether the individuals playing the recruiters let the conversational "opening" close up without acknowledging it in some way. Discuss some ideas for handling the situations mentioned in the ThinkAbout.

PEER AND GROUP DISCUSSION

ASK people to share their feelings about recruiting and working with people they know quite well.

Zero in on the pride they have in what they do, and **ASK** the group how this is transferable so that it can become a meaningful "gift" to give another person—stranger or friend.

Think About 11

Not everyone likes selling

Your beliefs are a part of who you are, what you say, and how you act. They simply can't be hidden.

If you believe in the value of what you do, it will show in the way you pay attention to details and the way you serve your customers and team. Your beliefs will be reflected in your accomplishments.

Your personal belief system is an essential part of the way you successfully recruit new people. It starts by generating curiosity when other people see the pride you have in your business leading to questions about what you do. If you are alert, it will help you start a discussion and direct it to the benefits, availability, and uniqueness of the opportunity you have to share.

And gradually as you talk about the service aspects of your business any negatives about selling will be erased.

Activator 11

WRITE

The following activities are concerned with how to dilute the negative feelings some people have about ***selling****.*

Think about the outstanding people you meet or hear about in your company. Develop a detailed list about what you feel motivates them to talk to prospects, make presentations, do demonstrations, express benefits, get orders and obtain referrals.

Now list how people who are negative about selling feel about the motives of people who sell. Can you find any of these motives on the first list you prepared? When you do, make a check mark. If your list is complete there will be a surprising number of the motives that will not be checked. What does that tell you?

SELF-ANALYSIS

Knowing that many people have reservations about selling, when someone asks you what you do, how do you answer? Do you say you're in sales (which is not very likely to generate interest, admiration, curiosity or discussion)? Or do you express excitement about what you do, how you help people, and hint at why what you do is so rewarding?

PEER OR GROUP DISCUSSION

Structure a discussion about how people feel about salespeople. What are the reasons they feel this way, why are these feelings inappropriate for what you do? What could you do to alleviate negative reactions when you are recruiting?

SHARE some experiences about personal contacts with different types of salespeople and include disappointments and successes.

DISCUSS how to deal with any anti-selling attitudes during the recruiting process.

Think About 12

Is the whole picture too big?

Sometimes the picture you paint for a potential recruit is too big to deal with or imagine.

When you don't know if you're talking to a Leader candidate, don't jump the gun and promote them before they've even begun.

Spell out what will happen step-by-step. Make beginning the new career a simple, step-by-step decision.

Use examples (with names) of people who felt like the potential recruit is feeling at the moment. Talk about their life changes and their successes.

Don't ask for lifetime decisions. Not yet. Simply ask for a decision to give the business a fair try for 30 or 60 days. What is an immediate goal to suggest? What needs to be done first?

Talk about "need-to-know" not "nice-to-know" and avoid information overload.

Sharing all of your knowledge is not as important as how much the newcomer to this "picture" can absorb.

Activator 12

TALK ABOUT

Are you a Leader? If you are, did you know when you were first recruited that you would be? Or did you come in part-time to test it out, and were pretty uncertain about your future role in the company? If you are not a Leader yet, do you want to be? What are you learning and feeling now about recruiting that will help you when you are working with new recruits?

SELF-EVALUATION

How do you feel about making decisions that involve time, people, money, your career, your working relationships, and the development of new skills, *yours and others?* Do you think your feelings are common or unique? What does it usually take to help you make a big decision when you are uncertain about what to do?

WRITE

Make a list of the decisions the potential recruit may be considering. Do you see these as big or little decisions? Why?

PEER OR GROUP DISCUSSION

COMPARE the lists of decisions. Agree which commitments are *little* decisions. On a step-by-step basis could these lead you to a firmer commitment from uncertain potential recruits?

DISCUSS some of the *little* things that may have kept previous recruits from making a *Yes* decision and anything that later changed their mind.

Think About 13

Watch out for the rocks!

Of all the rocks on the road to recruiting success, the biggest has to be when people feel negative about the idea of selling or being sold.

People don't say, "I'm going out buying." They say, "I'm going out shopping."

Who would want to be heard admitting,"I like to spend money," instead of "I'm exploring my shopping options?"

People don't really like to be sold on buying something. So they may hesitate about making commitments.

They are often wary about those who are trying to sell them something, even if they like the salesperson.

When you recognize this, you'll try harder to put more focus on the benefits and service of what you offer.

Doing this will help you to help people see you less as a *seller* and more as a *server*. You can turn rocks into pebbles with an attitude of service and caring.

And that's a good way to begin a relationship.

Think About 14

When enthusiasm is a disadvantage

It is good to be enthusiastic about your company and your business opportunity, but be temperate in your enthusiasm about the chances for someone's success if you sense any self-doubts.

When I feel you see in me things I'm not sure really exist, I may back away. I don't want to disappoint you or let you down by not meeting your expectations. This is no time for superlatives. It's the time for facts.

Relate *natural* skills or personal experience to what you do in a take-for-granted way. That way the prospect is more likely to understand that they can succeed and you're not just *selling*.

No one wants to be sold. When you are selling at your very best you are helping a person convince themselves to do something that is good for them.

The best way to get a firm footing is to tell some stories that make prospects think,"That's for me. I want that!" or "I could do that!" When you relate well with others, your enthusiasm is contagious.

Think About 15

Examine your feelings

Think about your subconscious, deep-down, hidden feelings about recruiting.

If you are not actively recruiting as a daily part of your business, there have to be some reasons.

To not try to understand what's happening in your head or your heart is like wearing a blindfold and trying to race up a twisting, steep hill to success.

To understand what motivates or inhibits you is to take off your blindfold so you can be free to run to the happy place where you are destined to be.

Don't let the race create pressure and stress. If you really believe in yourself, and in your goals and dreams, you won't be stressed. Stress comes from doubt.

Laugh a lot! Meetings and no-shows and people who don't do what they say they will are part of the price to pay and it is well worth it. So don't fret. Laugh and go on and grow!

What are you responsible for?

You are responsible to share your business opportunity and basic information with people.

You are responsible to offer guidance to launch a new business.

You are responsible to share the knowledge that you have learned to build a business.

You are responsible to answer questions that are asked by your team or to direct them to someone who can.

You are responsible to encourage your team to achieve more, to grow and stretch to become their best selves.

You are responsible to keep growing personally if you choose to become a great Leader.

You are responsible to point people toward information they want or need. You may direct them to the company website, customer service, training materials or to your Leader.

You are responsible to people, *but not* for their success or failure. Only they can decide to build and grow. It is not your responsibility to build their business for them.

Always keep recruiting

Why do new recruits fail? People fail if they don't learn the basic elements involved in the business or if they don't develop their people skills. This is not a classroom business.

People learn in 3 main ways.

1. By observation: watching a mentor or role model
2. By participation: personal practice
3. By presentation: doing what you need to do to get results such as sales, recruits or referrals, in tangible ways

The key to success in this business is consistency. If you do not work your company program properly, and consistently, you cannot expect your team to do any better. The program works if you work the program.

Be consistent in prospecting for new people to join you. Be business like, organized, and a good time manager. Be genuine and care about the people you meet and recruit.

There is no need to be perfect. There is a need to keep improving your skills and to follow the most basic rule of this business: Always keep recruiting.

18 - 31

Finding Prospects

Who do you know? 40
Everyone you know is qualified..................... 42
Do you have tunnel vision?............................ 43
Overlooking obvious prospects? 44
Think about products or services 46
Utilize the power of the phone 48
Using technology to recruit............................ 50
Going social – new tools of the trade 51
Be sure to walk through the door 52
Zero in when you hear a clue......................... 54
What about treasure hunts? 56
Motivation can be simple 57
Are you a rescuer? 58
Moving targets 60

Think About 18

Who do you know?

Who likes people, and is willing to learn, and who has done or said something that indicated a desire to grow?

Who do you know who likes, or has purchased, or is a prospect for whatever you offer?

Who do you know whose life has changed recently? Or who wants their life to change?

Who do you know who is successful and wants more?

Who do you know that you have never told about the many advantages of your own business or new career?

Who do you know who works for a company that rumor says is going to layoff, merge or downsize?

If you care enough to reach out and explore the interests, desires, and needs of these people, they could be your new recruits.

It's easier than you think. All you need to do is arouse their curiosity and suggest you have something to tell them that they will be very glad to hear.

Activator 18

WRITE

Divide a sheet of paper into seven wide columns with the ThinkAbout questions as headlines. See how many names you can list in answer to each of them. What other questions could you add to these? Write them out and do the same exercise, thinking of names to put under the headings. Think about the kind of people you want to grow with you.

SELF-ANALYSIS

Do you feel you've thought about these questions so many times that there is no need to rehash them now? Or do you know you can make the same kind of list many times and still discover you've forgotten to include people who should be on it? What kind of a system do you have for recording any name you happen to think of when you are on the run?

PEER AND GROUP DISCUSSION

PLAY the ABC game. Call out each letter. Then have the group answer with people or places to look for recruits that begin with the letter called. Tell them answers can be silly or sensible. For example, A could be aunts or attorneys or apple growers or ant killers. Get as many responses as you can for each letter of the alphabet. Keep the pace fast and enthusiastic. It may get noisy, but they'll get the idea that the lead potential is limitless. At another time do the same thing with the Yellow Pages or Chamber of Commerce directory. Go through the book to see how many businesses are reminders of someone to call for an appointment. **DISCUSS** the best places to look for recruits as well as the various methods for finding them. Consider one-on-one, group meetings, advertising, referrals, etc. Put the most emphasis on using referral techniques, the least emphasis on advertising.

Think About 19

Everyone you know is qualified

We need to realize the many ways life prepares us to be in sales. We are all qualified.

Every time we convince someone about something, such as where to go, what to buy, or even to get married, we are selling! Selling is simply *convincing*.

When people react negatively to the idea of selling, they are relating to a past experience with an offensive, pushy person who tried unsuccessfully to sell them something.

In contrast, in your business when you're convincing someone about things that have purpose, you're helping, you're serving, and you're assisting people in making a decision you honestly feel is good for them.

Whether you're talking to a top executive, someone who is in middle management, a couple, or a homemaker all you need is to be natural. Just be you!

People *sell* when they ask anyone for a decision about anything. So selling is a natural skill!

Think About 20

Do you have tunnel vision?

Is it possible that you feel so strongly about your reasons for getting in the business that you have tunnel vision about the motives of others?

If you were a stressed out executive, or unemployed, or a young woman seeing income possibilities, or a working mom who wanted to be home with your kids: your motivation may not have been the same, or the best, or the only motivation for others.

They may want money more than you did, a promotion and recognition, the trips, not being an employee anymore, or to get out of the house and spend more time talking with adults than small children.

If you wanted just a little extra income and then switched to full time when you saw the big picture, this does not mean that everyone has the same motivation.

Here's a rule to remember. *Assumption is the single biggest cause of communication breakdown.*

So in recruiting don't assume. Always explore.

Think About 21

Overlooking obvious prospects

It's as plain as the nose on your face!

This phrase is used when someone talks to someone else who can't find what they're looking for.

Fathers say it to sons who can't find the ball they are looking at or sometimes even holding. Every now and then we all tune out to what's around us.

That's why people sometimes hear about someone close to them who has recruited one of their business or social associates or even a family member.

Being close often breeds "clue-blindness."

So one of the first places to seek new recruit potential is in a long list of everyone you know. Be sure to list all your connections and all the places you spend money for goods and services.

Look and listen for the clues that are likely to motivate people to take the time to listen to what you have to say.

And if they aren't interested, be sure to ask them to refer you to people they know.

Activator 21

TALK ABOUT

Have you ever looked for something and then discovered you'd looked right at it several times and didn't see it? Has this ever happened to you with a potential recruit? Do you think it is possible this happened to you and you didn't realize it?

SELF-EVALUATION

Even though it sounds silly to acknowledge that it's possible you sometimes don't see what's in front of you, are you willing to admit it can happen? If you don't want to admit this, why are you so sure you're always aware and tuned in to what's around you?

Have you ever heard someone you know joined a Direct Sales company and it had never occurred to you to tell them about your opportunity? Do you know if anyone you know has been recruited by someone else into your company? How do you or would you feel about it? Would you change who you approach? What else would you do differently?

PEER AND GROUP DISCUSSION

ASK which people close to us are we most likely to overlook as potential recruits? Who do you know who has probably never overlooked a potential recruit? What do they do that you don't? How did you get into the business? Did you recruit yourself or did someone make an effort to convince you of the opportunity?

Who has an idea about how we can begin to increase our level of awareness, so we don't overlook the potential recruits who are right under our noses?

Think About 22

Think about products or services

Who likes or appreciates or uses your products or your service? Consider all these people as potential recruits!

What you need to do now is be generous by sharing ideas, and wise enough to study and practice good approaches.

Don't assume interest in your business just because there is an interest in your product or service. Interest is simply an open door. It'll lead you where you want to go.

Be sensitive to your audience as you go through the door and move to the business opportunity. People are bound to be skeptical about their abilities and new choices.

Focus on how they feel about the decision they made to buy and the reason they said *Yes*. It's a reflection of their good feelings toward you and your company.

The potential recruits will then be able to relate their own feelings to how others might feel, and this will help open their minds to the potential of your business.

Focus on the company and your support system, the excitement, rewards, recognition and even the joy and sense of achievement to add appeal.

Activator 22

WRITE

Make a list of at least five reasons (related only to what and how you sell) that a customer might be a prospective recruit.

SELF-ANALYSIS

How many of your last ten customers did you try to recruit either by a direct approach or by asking for referrals? Can you think of any logical reason for not offering the career opportunity to every customer at the time of purchase or during a follow-up call? If you showed these reasons to your Leader, can you guess what the reaction would be? If you can't guess the reaction, are you willing to review your list with your Leader to find out if you agree and if your reasons have any validity? In your list, did your five reasons include: familiarity, belief in value, useful, solves a problem, acceptance of need, respect for your company and respect for you?

ROLE-PLAY

Take turns describing and role-playing getting an appointment to talk about the business with a customer. After the role-play, analyze and discuss the customer's feelings and probable reaction.

PEER AND GROUP DISCUSSION

Pass out blank sheets of paper. Ask everyone to write three figures in a vertical line. 1. The number of customers they've had contact with in the last month. 2. The number of those customers that they tried to recruit. 3. How many of these customers were asked for referrals. Discuss the differences in the numbers and talk about changing these results this month.

Think About 23

Utilize the power of the phone

Some people you know live too far away for you to meet with them so they can see exactly what you do, but that certainly doesn't mean they should be excluded.

When used properly, the phone is a powerful long distance recruiting tool. You do need to offer good service, follow-up, and training. The phone can save you time!

Work hard practicing "your script" until what you say sounds natural so you will get results. Then schedule a block of time for non-stop calling.

Sales research proves that your phone selling efficiency usually increases the second hour of calling. Momentum helps build the ratio of *Yes* over *No* responses.

Making calls and then stopping to do something else is not what phone marketing is all about.

It's about making call after call with a long list of contacts, questions to ask, and an outline of what you intend to say. Also know how you will handle any resistance.

Capitalize on phone power. It's a practical way to recruit, and if not, to get sales, appointments, or referrals!

Activator 23

TALK ABOUT

Who do you keep in touch with by phone, e-mail, texting or Facebook? Who do you know that you have not connected with in years? Who do you know from school or the old neighborhood? Do you receive holiday cards from people you hardly ever see? Who do you know from a former job in another city? What are these people doing now? Wouldn't you like to know? Wouldn't they like to know that about you?

WRITE

Start a name inventory of everyone you can think of who is out of your area. Don't label people. Don't make judgments. Just list names. If they aren't interested, they may have referrals. So write any name you can think of ASAP. Don't worry if you haven't heard from them in years. Think how pleased you'd be if someone remembered you and was curious about how you are and what you are doing. Add more names, and always keep adding to this list!

SELF-ANALYSIS

Is it possible you aren't sure whether they'd remember you or care you called? Are you afraid of seeming pushy? Do you know that when people are genuinely excited they sound enthusiastic? Ask yourself, what do you have to lose or gain? What is the worst that can happen? Is doing it worth it?

PEER AND GROUP DISCUSSION

Who has some experience recruiting over the phone? Does anyone you know have a phone presentation to share? What about phone recruiting experiences? Who would be willing to help you polish a presentation? What tools does the company provide to help you?

Think About 24

Using technology to recruit

Have you noticed how technology has impacted your business in the last five years? It's time to adapt. We now can recruit anywhere at any time of day or night.

Twenty five years ago, 3-way calling came into existence and became a time saver in connecting and training. It's still a great way to support your team and speak to their prospects with them across town or across the country.

Just a dozen years ago, we shared a cassette tape or a VHS video and asked someone to listen or watch and then call us. Next came CDs and DVDs. Today you can send an MP3 message by e-mail or text and your company or Leader likely offers a recruiting call recorded for access 24/7.

You may be able to send people to your company website to view the opportunity in an interactive webinar. They sign into your personal website and you get an e-mail to follow up with them.

How about Skype? Have you engaged a prospect face to face on your desktop, laptop, notebook or cell phone? Our world keeps getting smaller as technology continues to advance. Connect with the people in your company that use the tools available and learn how to enjoy the convenience of connecting quickly and easily.

Think About 25

Going social – new tools of the trade

Direct Selling is the original social media. This business model has spread by word of mouth for over 100 years. It has always been about sharing to enhance the lives of the people we know and to meet the people they know, through referrals.

Social is the new buzzword for connecting and forming relationships. Social media affects us every day. Get comfortable with it and embrace it.

We have more contact with more people today, than ever before. We create social relationships, social commerce, social giving, social everything.

Have you explored the possibilities of Facebook? Do you have a business page? How about Twitter? Have you used 140 characters to recognize someone or to give customers reasons to join your company? Do you link with others on LinkedIn to enhance your professional relationships?

Do you participate in any Blogs from industry Leaders and speakers or in company forums to share business building tips?

Now is the time to go social! The social marketplace will continue to expand. Be a part of it!

Think About 26

Be sure to walk through the door

If someone is going to open a door for you, wouldn't you want to be prepared to walk through it comfortably, especially if you knew it would lead to an opportunity?

Think about the times you've been asked the *door-opener* question; "What do you do for a living?" Were you prepared to respond in an effective way?

Wouldn't it be smart to have a short *commercial* developed to make the prospect curious? It could be as simple as, "I show people how to ___". And then you'd add whatever you like best about what you do.

Your response should be concise and intriguing. It should create curiosity, the first step in getting an appointment, so you can talk about your company in more detail.

Or if the situation is inappropriate for recruiting, you can say something like, "I'm really excited about what I do. I'll call you. We'll have coffee soon so I can tell you about it."

Or answer, and then say something that works like a question,"Tell me more about you, Mary."

It's simple to hear clues about how what you offer can fit the questioner's particular life situation and open a door.

Activator 26

TALK ABOUT

What situations have you been in been in recently where there were probably some potential recruits? How often do people ask you what you do or what you've been up to lately? If you don't get the question, what can you do to encourage it? What happens when you ask,"What do you do?"

WRITE

Pretend you are a very high-priced copywriter. Your assignment is to write in fifty words or less what you do to earn a second income or as your full-time career. Keep in mind that professional copywriters write, rewrite, edit and polish, so that the words are powerful and there are no wasted or meaningless words. Read your "commercial" out loud. Talk to yourself as you look in the mirror. Do you sound natural? Can you say it without looking at the words? Do you feel it will serve your purpose because most people will be curious? Are you comfortable saying it?

PEER OR GROUP DISCUSSION

Have everyone write a *commercial* in the next 5-10 minutes. If you have weekly or monthly meetings, ask attendees to bring their written and practiced *commercial* to the next meeting. Have individuals present their *commercials.* Have the group talk about their reactions. Then vote by applause for the best three. Try some group role-play and feedback. Always have the person who wrote the *commercial* give their feedback first, then the group. The meeting Leader wraps up with a recap of ideas.

Think About 27

Zero in when you hear a cue

When you hear about a need for money to do something, or to buy something extra special, or to cover expenses - those are cues. Act now!

Get a date to talk soon, within 24 to 48 hours. Don't file the name away to call later. The situation may change and you may miss a natural opportunity.

While the need is hot and urgent, fan the flames. Reach out with a solution for the current problem. Demonstrate how helping solve problems is an essential and satisfying part of your business.

Be specific about the simple steps to learn the business and about time involvement and rewards.

When people have needs or troubles, it may be difficult for them to see help and not feel that they are *dreaming the rescue.* What they hear may seem too good to be true.

To be convincing, talk specifically about what can be done. Later you can relate very realistically to their dreams about their future.

Right now a practical approach is best.

Activator 27

TALK ABOUT

What does a *cue* mean to *you*? Does it mean someone has given you an opening to say something? As you read the ThinkAbout, did any memories about not picking up on a cue flash through your mind? If they did, try to look back and see if examining the past can teach you anything helpful you can apply in the future.

SELF-MOTIVATOR

Set yourself a measurable goal to find X number of potential recruits to talk to in the next two weeks. In each case, make up your mind you are going to offer the opportunity as the answer to fill a definite need. Watch for cues (obvious) and clues (subtle).

PEER OR GROUP DISCUSSION

ASK: You hear cues that indicate immediate needs in a variety of situations. Can you think of any past experiences where cues might have led you to a new recruit? What happened? Looking back what would you do differently?

What do you think is meant by *dreaming the rescue*? Has this happened when you shared the business opportunity with someone? What do you do when something seems too good to be true? What are the steps a potential recruit should be told about in order to feel comfortable about learning and the support process?

Think About 28

What about treasure hunts?

A treasure hunt is a fun party activity where people are given obscure clues to look for things difficult to find.

Given even the vaguest of clues, persistency usually pays off, because these people search, ask, seek and try.

And eventually a surprising number find exactly what they are looking for, and end up being winners.

Is the reason you don't recruit enough, that you don't have the clues spelled out?

Do you see the clue, but give up too soon?

Do you fail to recognize a clue is not always what it seems, but is really another clue for you to take an entirely different direction?

Is it possible you don't see the fun and efficiency in using clues to help you recruit?

Think About 29

Motivation can be simple

To encourage yourself to do anything, you need to have a real *Why* (a compelling reason, something you want out of your business), and it needs to be defined clearly in writing, as a meaningful objective.

Your personal *Why* should be something you really want to accomplish, to be, to do, to have, or to give.

To be meaningful, an objective needs to be specific, (with a time frame), measurable (with a number), realistic (able to be achieved), and challenging (a bit of a stretch). What is your current objective? Is it in writing? Have you shared it with someone?

You don't diet to not eat. You diet to improve your health, to be a smaller size, or just to feel better.

You don't recruit just to compete or to show-off your growing numbers or income.

So, to motivate yourself, decide what you want now and what you want to build. Do you recruit because you want to be proud of your own business and how it is growing?

And at the same time, wouldn't you feel good when you recruit knowing you're helping others?

Think About 30

Are you a rescuer?

If someone were yelling out for help, would you reach out and give the person a helping hand?

What if someone was just barely whimpering, much too embarrassed to ask for your help? Would your reaction be the same?

Assume they are not endangered, but if you do not offer help the person may be stuck where they are indefinitely.

What would you do? If your efforts to set the person free were successful, how would you feel?

Naturally, it's possible you could fail and be disappointed and maybe frustrated.

But because you didn't save a particular recruit who really needed cash or the choices the business could offer, would you let that keep you from reaching out to help someone else?

Is there ever any reason to deny help to someone?

Activator 30

TALK ABOUT

What are some of the things people do that get in the way of your sensing clues and learning if a person is a prospect?

WRITE

Make a list of your worst communication faults, things that get in the way of hearing your prospect's whole story and sensing the cues in it. For example, do you often interrupt because you are overly enthusiastic about making a point or because you're certain you know what the person is going to say or ask, and you want to save time? Do you listen intensely or halfway tune out because you're planning what to say next?

SELF MOTIVATION

Promise yourself a reward if, by playing *clue-detector*, you discover three clues during the next week which, in talking to three potential recruits, were not expressed or obvious.

PEER OR GROUP DISCUSSION

What if you knew nothing about someone, except that they seem to like your product or service, or want extra money or a new career? What questions would you ask to explore their recruit potential? It's important to get cues or clues to use in your approach and later in the interview, at the same time keeping your motives less apparent.

DISCUSS how to avoid talking over people (a bad habit), by inserting silence to make certain they've said everything they wanted to say.

TALK ABOUT counting 1-2-3 silently before responding. Provide structure by telling prospects "This is what I want to accomplish in the next X minutes." Get feedback by asking open-ended questions that can't be answered with *Yes* or *No*.

Think About 31

Moving Targets

There are plenty of motivational speakers who tell us to always wear our *happy face* and *think positive,* and that's usually good advice to share.

Are we being brainwashed not to worry, and if we do worry, to never ever let it show?

Plenty of things make us aware we shouldn't place our worries on someone else's back and to just have faith that we can work to make ourselves better.

So the clues you seek are about money worries, boredom, lack of recognition, crummy job, and the awful feeling of not achieving anything worthwhile. These clues are seldom going to be paraded before you like ducks in a shooting gallery, where practice will make you a better shot at your target.

In recruiting, more than likely, you're dealing with shadows that move and hide in the dark.

Clues about feelings, worries and life situations seldom shout for recognition. They're usually hidden.

But by fine-tuning your empathy skills you'll often be able to detect feelings and sense problems as you project potential.

32 - 42

Finding More Prospects

Making extra money is OK 62
Working with a reluctant prospect 63
Are they limiting themselves? 64
Being shy can be an asset................................. 65
We only go through life once 66
What you see is what you get! 67
What happens when I'm not new? 68
There is pain in being on a plateau 69
I don't see myself as a Team Leader 70
Consider the watermelon 71
Think of recruiting as courtship 72

Think About 32

Making extra money is OK

Does making money because of other's work mentally get in the way of your recruiting?

IF you feel guilty, don't! The protocol of business everywhere is to reward the Leaders.

If you lead someone to a method of earning money and finding fulfillment, plus a way to get their efforts recognized, you are entitled to rewards.

Any company is delighted to share earnings with those who help them build their business.

Your recruits know this instinctively. Anything else just wouldn't make sense. Understand this.

Don't focus on the generous return on your time investment. Expect and be grateful for it.

Applaud your ability and willingness to help others find what they are looking for: money, time, or a brighter future.

Think About 33

Working with a reluctant prospect

There are people who back away from saying *Yes* because they simply cannot imagine making money by selling to friends, relatives and neighbors. They aren't sure where else to find their first prospects.

Help them change their emphasis!

They're focusing on what they stand to gain, and they feel this will be obvious. That's why they don't want to be seen as a pushy salesperson that is "using" a friend.

Ask questions: What if they knew a better doctor, a better supermarket, a great restaurant, a fabulous movie or a really exciting book, would they keep it secret?

Wouldn't the same hold true about an easier way to earn money by working flexible hours that fit varying life styles?

What about a way to "job-test" and not have to interfere with or leave a regular job?

Shouldn't you feel that people you know and like are entitled to hear the good news?

Think About 34

Are they limiting themselves?

Is someone not recruiting because they fear failure? You're not likely to hear the words "I'm afraid that I would fail!"

Instead what you hear is "That's not for me," or "I could never do that," or "I'm not interested in recruiting."

You do the person a disservice if you settle for what they say. Instead respond and react to what is really meant by their words.

If you sense fear of failure, talk about the flexible support system and how it will work for the person with whom you are talking.

Focus on the importance of trying and that no matter what happens the time invested has a pay off.

Be specific about the benefits of the experience and learning, even when the answer is no.

Be reassuring and be specific. Generalities are not likely to work as well as offering to help them reach out to recruit someone they think might do well.

Talk about being partners and then really be one!

Think About 35

Being shy can be an asset

When you are proficient at what you do, potential recruits might think or say, "I could never do that like you do it!" or "I'm not interested in doing what you do."

You usually recognize shyness, so tune into the expected before the negative is expressed. But if it's expressed, do have a comeback ready to use. Try something like this:

"There is something that crossed my mind that I should have told you. It's about why you may be better at this business than I am."

You've aroused curiosity. Bet on it! Go on and explain.

"When I say 'hello' because I am so naturally enthusiastic, it often sounds like I am selling the day. But some people just don't believe that my enthusiasm is real."

"You are quieter and more comfortable to listen to than I am and as a result you'll have greater credibility and are bound to do well."

After recruiting, warn them not to catch S.N.I.O.P. which stands for the Subtle Negative Influence of Other People.

Think About 36

We only go through life once

In life it is a privilege when we contribute to helping people to be happy and successful.

As you reach out to someone when you are recruiting, you are touching and changing lives.

The personal growth, the extra money, and the personal and financial rewards of your business touch more than the person you recruit.

Your success, achievement, and joy, touches families, friends, partners, and of course, the children who will learn things about goals they may never learn in school.

It's like you're dropping a pebble in a lake and watching ripples spreading out, expanding the effect of your meaningful action, your recruiting effort.

Don't just stand on the shore of opportunity where the view is so lovely and not make the effort to reach out and invite someone to share it.

Think About 37

What you see is what you get!

There is a space in a person's mind that they fill with one of two things. They either fill it with zeros, negative feelings, and lots of pessimism and fear of what they don't want. Or, they fill it with numbers, positive feelings, hopes, dreams, wishes, and optimism for what they do want.

You get to decide what will fill your space. It's up to you to determine how your thoughts and beliefs will influence your life and your recruiting efforts...positively or negatively. You choose!

Changing the way you see things can change your attitude, ambitions and self awareness, and in the process change your life.

Is your glass half-full or half-empty?

Do you see potential recruits almost everywhere? Or do you have a hard time identifying any recruits at all?

If you don't see potential recruits in your daily activities, is it possible that you are deliberately blinding yourself to opportunity and success?

Can you focus on how you will benefit, and also on how sharing your opportunity benefits others?

Think About 38

What happens when I'm not new?

Chances are you're wondering about one of two things; "How good am I going to be doing this on my own?" and "What am I going to do when the newness wears off and I've approached almost everyone I know?"

Good for you for asking these key questions. They relate to building and protecting your business by consistent recruiting or what we call maintaining momentum.

If you follow the pattern of the people in your business who are working the business successfully, you will soon discover a very simple process creates growth.

Scheduling time for consistent recruiting is the only way to keep your business fresh and growing.

It's like a garden. Your new recruits are your seedlings. With initial training you and your mentor nourish them and get them ready to sprout. Suddenly they are blooming and growing!

By watching, tending, and offering support consistently, you make your recruits strong and become better at what you do. It's as simple as that, but if you don't, seedlings can just wither away!

Think About 39

There is pain in being on a plateau

If you are planning to travel fast and far there is no way to assure you there will be no bumps on the road, no sudden unexpected turns and no plateaus where you feel stuck.

We can assure you, things will or won't happen, it's a given. How you react, well that's something you choose.

Have you heard the saying, "Attitude is everything?" It is hard to argue that because attitude influences every single part of your life. When things don't go perfectly, having the right attitude to be able to work yourself through the rough spots is your best asset.

The really tough part is feeling you've been working hard and, suddenly, nothing is going right. After climbing in sales and income, you hit a plateau and discover who you are.

Yes, you may get disappointed by some people. But balancing that out is the number of people who will surprise you by going places you never imagined they could reach.

It's easier to get discouraged than it is to have hope and faith. There are only so many cards in a deck. When you hang in there and keep playing, you'll eventually get a better deal with winning cards. Or you'll start again working smart instead of just hard.

Think About 40

I don't see myself as a Team Leader

There are two replies to this comment depending on how long you've been in your business. If you are fairly new the response would be "Of course you don't."

If you are working with someone who is more experienced than you are, you may be wondering when you will catch up. It will be sooner than you think. Everything we do, or use, is designed to be duplicatible, including building teams.

If you have been in business a while and you have recruited a few people, the response would be; "You are already learning how to lead a team." You give help and guidance, alone or with your mentor. Team Leaders help people get started and support their objectives.

While you may not have thought about it, you have probably been acting like a Team Leader most of your life, as a sibling, parent, teacher, boss, or good friend.

Think about playing as a child and getting other children to play with you in a game. Think about putting together a group picnic, a meeting, a meal, or anything requiring working with other people in a supportive way. If you like people, get satisfaction in helping them do things, and praise their efforts, you already have the heart of a Team Leader. Building your team will be even simpler for you.

Think About 41

Consider the watermelon

Think about a delicious watermelon on a hot and humid day or as a surprising, delicious winter treat.

There's just one problem. To enjoy the watermelon you have to deal with the seeds. And seeds are a nuisance.

They get in the way when you're hungry or in a hurry. They slow down your progress in enjoying the fruit.

So ask yourself this; "Would you want to give up the delight of eating the watermelon just because of the seeds?"

Should you give up recruiting because you've found some bad seeds in your organization, people who weren't what they seemed to be?

Always remember, recruiting has nothing to do with perfection.

Some people aren't what they seem to be. Some will slow you down and take up your time. Understand this to get through the minor frustrations to enjoy the fruits of your efforts.

Is it worth it? Should we accept the seeds as part of the process? Yes we should! Why not?

Think About 42

Think of recruiting as courtship

Recruiting involves all the elements of a courtship.

It starts with a vision of something we care about and want in our life. That's when the steps of courtship begin.

The first step is intriguing.

This is the get acquainted process where we find out what we have in common, what appeals to us, and whether we want to see more of each other?

The next step is romancing.

This is the convincing process where we get to know each other better and see if we offer mutual benefits.

The third step is commitment.

This is where the long term relationship begins.

How long it lasts depends on the recruit's intellectual and emotional involvement and your commitment of support.

The question is, "Are your intentions honorable?"

43 - 51

Making Connections

Connecting with people 74
Life is about convincing 75
Understand their vantage point 76
Are you speaking their language? 77
Communication is mathematical 78
I don't know the right words 79
When you don't know what to say 80
If you won't ask for a decision 81
Are people who they seem to be? 82

Think About 43

Connecting with people

A Connector has synergistic interests. They see needs and matches, and help people connect with people of similar interests. They champion causes and find people to connect to ideas. You are, or you can grow to be, a connector. We all can. We learn how by observing them.

Connectors ask lots of questions out of genuine interest. They take time to find out about family, jobs, hopes, and dreams. They follow up; they might mail you a clipping or refer you to an internet site you'd love to see.

Connectors have great memories or great records which enable them to know what people do, to match them with others who need their product or service. They are great people to go to for referrals. Because of their synergistic nature they will love this business. Share it in terms of how you connect ideas and help people.

Connectors are achievers and know the difference between objectives and goals. When you share your business you gift them with meaningful objectives. Help them set new and exciting goals. Your original connectors create a cycle of success and continuous growth. Your team will grow faster than usual as they attract more synergistic connectors and business will be more fun and productive.

Connect to communicate. Connect with connectors to grow!

Think About 44

Life is about convincing

From the time we started crying in our cribs to convince our parents we needed attention we've spent much of our lives convincing someone about something.

Convincing skills come naturally.

We are all involved in convincing to one degree or another every day of our lives, even when we talk to ourselves.

Some people are naturally better at convincing than others, but the more we do it the better we get.

When a woman wants a new couch she doesn't need, or her husband wants to go golfing on their anniversary, convincing skills are needed.

That's one of the bonuses of this business. You learn the methods of being a more effective communicator and a more efficient convincer. This is a valuable asset in all areas of your life.

Keep practicing your recruiting skills and see how your business and your life improve!

Think About 45

Understand their vantage point

It's a mystery why one of the most essential rules of good communication is often forgotten because of who we are and what we personally think and care about.

Anyone who writes advertisements would fail if they had not been taught expressing their personal vantage point gets in the way of effective communication.

You see and hear it all the time. When an ad says "We are excited to introduce ____" it's not nearly as effective as saying; "You're going to be excited because _____." (Add a specific offer.)

Anyone who is married knows the big difference between saying; "I want "or "I need" versus "You are going to love it when ___." The difference in vantage points is enormous.

There are all kinds of communication situations in your life when there is absolutely no way to know what the other person is thinking. You have only two appeals for attention that will work: curiosity and sense of personal benefit.

Whether you are talking or writing, express what you say or ask from the vantage point of your audience. You will find this almost always creates curiosity or a feeling that whatever you're talking about might benefit them. This rule is infallible. For better connections, follow it!

Think About 46

Are you speaking their language?

Have you ever been in a situation when you could not find the right words? While this is not uncommon it is certainly uncomfortable. Often we need more than words.

Chances are you couldn't find the right *feelings* to reach out and connect. This is important to any communication situation. It is essential to choose your words to evoke emotions.

To communicate you must accept the responsibility for creating mutual interest and benefits. You cannot communicate if you and the person with whom you are speaking are on different tracks.

You develop real communication and make a connection by asking questions.

If you are curious about someone and how they feel, then you are talking on the same track. Show genuine interest in them. Find common ground.

Questions reveal feelings and interests, which can lead you to the language of their heart and find out what makes it sing.

Pay attention and listen carefully. Find a way to connect emotionally. Try to really understand how someone feels. If you cannot connect emotionally maybe you should move on.

Think About 47

Communication is mathematical

If you apply the principles of arithmetic to the way you talk to people you want to cross ***division*** off the list.

You don't want any communication you are involved in to ***subtract*** from something that exists unless, of course, it eliminates a negative or reduces a problem.

Multiplication is fine if we are talking about words, or about a good or strong message needing to be sent, not just to one person, but to many people.

Addition is wonderful! It's what recruiting is all about and should be addictive. It's a habit that builds businesses.

What you say and do can mathematically subtract from or add to growth and future income. Add continuous education to develop your ability to find, coach, support, and help others grow.

To be successful in a sharing business, be constantly aware of your personal growth. Every now and then measure the value of what you're doing.

People skills are an asset that grows in value as you and your team learn more about reaching out to share. Leverage time and talent regularly to add to your personal riches.

Think About 48

I don't know the right words

Isn't it interesting when someone finds out that what they do poorly in one situation is actually their strength in another?

It is important for you to recognize in any business situation there are certain powerful words, that when added to natural conversations usually increase your odds of good results.

Remember, during the recruiting process you are sharing, not selling, and you should be talking to people in a natural way. Every now and then insert "power words." There are five power words that really work. One is LOVE (People love to ___). Another is EVERYONE (Everyone on our team does ___, or Everyone I've talked to agrees that___.)

Another powerful word is ALL (All the things we do are simple to learn.) ALWAYS has a powerful impact, it reflects continuity (Our most successful people always ___.)

Most people like consistency, so saying EVERY reflects assurance. It's a word that conveys a sense of normalcy. (I offer to share ___ with every person I meet, every day.") Along with power words, your attitude and your joy in being able to present something you believe in creates connection. Choose the right words and you will be convincing.

Think About 49

When you don't know what to say

Famous singers, comedians and talk show hosts do a lot of rehearsing to sound casual, so why shouldn't you? Especially when you know exactly the situations in which you are going to initiate conversation or respond to questions.

Think of 10 or 30 second commercials on TV and radio, they say a lot. So can you, sharing your person-to-person commercial. For example; "How many things can you say that begin with "I show people how to ____."

Don't hesitate to ask for advice. Most people are likely to be flattered when you say "I would appreciate your advice. I am looking for someone successful who wants more financial security or who wants to find a way to use their skills. Can you think of anyone?"

Your company has training on what to say and ask. Talk with successful people. They love to help other people grow. It's a good feeling to contribute to another person's success. That's why many choose our sharing business.

The very best advice is to forget about selling or that you are earning money. Instead focus on the fact you are offering an opportunity to someone whose life you could change. Someone else may talk to your relatives or neighbors about their opportunities. They will wonder why you didn't tell them about yours. Understand why you didn't.

Think About 50

If you won't ask for a decision...

Take time out to evaluate what happened. Why were you talking to this person? What was your real objective?

Did you want to look like you were busy working? This does happen and it's a mammoth barrier to success. It fools no one, especially you.

Do you ever schedule meetings just to say you *talked to someone?* Have you ever thought if you meet with someone, they might just ask to join your business?

Begin with the reality of what you have to offer, why it's valuable and why you want and need to schedule your time wisely.

Is it possible you are not always prepared to sign up your prospect to join your team and company?

If you don't keep marketing material handy (in your briefcase or car) do you realize this definitely indicates you're not prepared either emotionally or physically to get a decision?

If you are not going to ask for a decision, don't waste time, theirs and yours. If this happens, and it might, don't let this opportunity to learn what happened pass you by. Talk to your mentor. One of best ways to grow is to analyze what went wrong and why.

Think About 51

Are people who they seem to be?

People you know who appear assertive, out-going, and sure of themselves, may be filled with more doubts and insecurities than the shyest person you know.

In psychology this is called "reaction formation." And it can fool very wise and discerning people.

So when recruiting out-going personalities, don't assume you won't have to deal with doubts and fears.

Instead be sure to build into your recruiting conversations information about the law of averages, the key steps to success, and the on-going support.

This kind of person needs to hear things that will assure them that they won't be thrown in the water until they are certain they can "swim safely".

When recruiting, improve your results by learning to deal with a variety of personalities.

Be flexible. Keep learning. Know the way people act is not always a true picture of who they are or how they feel.

Knowledge and flexibility increase results!

52 - 60

Developing Relationships

Breaking down the barriers 84
Presenting your company story 85
What to do instead of sell 86
"It's good for you" does not work 87
Two very powerful questions 88
Flush out the zinger 89
Never be lonely again 90
When you build people, they build business 91
Do you know what motivates me? 92

Think About 52

Breaking down the barriers

Good recruiters read books, listen to MP3s, participate in webinars and conference calls to observe and absorb what the successful say. They duplicate what works.

But until you make another's words your own and use them in your talking style, they just won't work.

Some may have tried their own business before and may have been led astray by false promises or may have been psychologically or financially hurt or disappointed.

Your approach may have to break down the barriers of personal doubts and bad experiences.

Rehearse an approach script and change words slightly to suit your style. Talk out loud into a mirror until you know you can say what you want to say without looking at the script.

Talk out loud until you know what you say sounds like your own natural conversational style.

Barriers won't fall if you don't sound like yourself.

Think About 53

Presenting your company story

When you are ready to give a presentation or interview, it's Show time! The curtain is going up when you are ready to talk about your business.

This is a key moment in recruiting.

This is where rehearsal and practice pay off. It is where you get the applause (a *Yes*), or you lose the audience (a *No*), or you get something in between (a *maybe* or *not right now*).

This is where your audience decides if you are worth seeing again, because they are interested in what you showed and/or told them or because they like your style.

The price of their ticket is their time. Now the decision is whether to invest more time or walk away.

It's not always easy to be on center stage, but it's a lot easier when you know you are prepared to do your best because you have invested your time and learned what works best from your Leaders and mentors.

Preparation makes people stars. Understanding resistance builds relationships.

Good presentations get decisions and commitments.

Think About 54

What to do instead of sell

You'll be more comfortable in any presentation situation when you are telling and not selling.

So get rid of the old sales language in your head. It doesn't belong in your vocabulary anymore. Be contemporary!

Focus on helping, not pushing.

When you sell you are under pressure to *close*. When you tell, you are explaining something appealing you want listeners to understand so they will be enthusiastic about wanting to make a *commitment* to get involved with you and what you offer.

You don't have to *handle objections*. If your program is right, there's nothing to object to. But it's only natural to have to *deal with resistance.*

Incidentally, remember there will rarely be any resistance you shouldn't expect. There are few surprises.

Get rid of expected resistance up front. If you know I'm likely to say "I'm busy," say, "I want to talk to you. You're the busiest person I know." Think ahead to get ahead!

Think About 55

"It's good for you" does not work

Remember when you were a child and someone told you to eat your vegetables? Maybe you didn't like vegetables. Was it because someone else (perhaps a sibling) didn't like them?

Or maybe it was because you were told so often, "It's good for you!" that you just wanted to scream.

Would it have been different if there had been some pleasant conversation about the delicious flavor or the texture?

Is it possible in your business you hear so often that recruiting is *good for you* that you end up seeing the *task* instead of the *reward*?

Is it possible you are less motivated by something you're told you *have to do* and this blinds you to obvious gain?

The solution is to focus on the benefits, the personal gain. Doing this may make it easier to get started and to keep going.

Why not begin to think of recruiting as a really scrumptious dessert you want to enjoy?

Think About 56

Two very powerful questions

When you've talked about your opportunity to someone who is not interested ask; "Who do you know who would **appreciate being alerted** to this opportunity to_____?"

You'll get a double take because of the positive belief that the question reflects. You'll earn attention because of the three bold "triggers" (words that get attention).

And then you will very likely get some new referral names. Use the question and keep track of results. Discover how well the question works when you use the exact words.

Or try the "Colombo Approach." Seem to accept a *No* and get up to leave. Before going out the door, come back and sit down or stand near the person. Put your materials down saying, "I have one question I just have to ask you."

Quietly, slowly, and sincerely ask, "If you knew as much about (Name of the Company) as I do, and if you felt as strongly as I do that (Name of the Company) would be right for you, what would you have said or done differently, that I didn't do?"

Then be still and let silence work for you.

Think About 57

Flush out the zinger

You've been given a format or process for a *recruiting approach* and for a *presentation or interview* by your company. You know how important it is to build rapport. You gather information about people by asking questions.

When you approach someone, give enough info about you and what you do to build curiosity to know more. In a presentation you share your business story.

When you meet with someone, realize many people already have a reason in mind for not joining your business. You need to know what it is so you can get in front of it, so it doesn't become a barrier to a *Yes!*

For example, you might ask, "(NAME), before I tell you the benefits about what I do, I have one more question. If you like what you hear today, is there anything that would keep you from getting started right now?"

Don't comment on it, just say, "Thanks for sharing that." Remember it. When you present the opportunity, address the resistance to reduce its power and flush out the zinger to get a *Yes!*

Think About 58

Never be lonely again

One of the blessings of having a home based business is that you'll never be lonely. There is always somebody to see or someone you can call.

There is always someone you could reach out to help. Or you can call someone to get help for yourself. They'll be pleased and often honored that you asked.

You have choices. You can sit in front of your TV or you can go explore your company website. Listen to success stories and explore business building ideas. Learn and take action, try it and see. You can go to places where people are looking for work and find prospects. When you're busy, your chances for success increase. If you are busy at the right things your income will also increase.

You have such a natural conversation starter. You have a reason to talk to strangers. You know who you're looking for. Say; "I have a hunch about you, I'm doing something I feel you might be interested in." Then set an appointment to meet. You have the privilege to make people feel good when you reach out and talk with them. The possibilities are endless! If you are ever lonely, it's by your own choosing.

Think About 59

When you build people, they build business

As you build a team, you learn how to work with many personalities and bring out the best in people. Your skills expand through interaction with people from different places, backgrounds, levels of education and desires. Actually Direct Sales is the great equalizer, no prior experience is necessary. Everyone who joins has the same opportunity to succeed and their level of success depends on their personal efforts and actions.

If you desire to succeed at the highest level of your company plan, it's important for you to develop a large and successful team. Building people requires communication, connection, recognition, goal setting and stretching to continually achieve more.

Connect on a personal as well as a business level. Take time to find out about their family, jobs, hopes, wishes and dreams. Recognize people for taking the right actions to grow. Set goals with them for what they want to achieve in sales, recruiting and Leadership, and then celebrate with them when they achieve their goal.

Most importantly, when they achieve anything, challenge them to reset their goals to strive for more. Create a cycle of success and continuous growth for yourself and for your people and your business will always be moving forward.

Think About 60

Do you know what motivates me?

If I know you are trying to recruit me, and if something would motivate me to say *Yes*! to your offer, I may not want you to know what it is.

Even though you may suspect what it is, will I tell you if you're right? Of course not! I will come up with excuses, doubts and logical sounding rationalizations.

I will work so hard at not letting you convince me, that I'll hardly hear the appealing facts you are presenting.

The key to the challenge of clue-catching is not what you say to try to flush out the positive responses or the fresh clues. It is in the questions you ask.

You need thoughtful questions that simply can't be answered with a *Yes* or *No* response. You want feedback and clues.

Ask questions to allow the potential recruit to feel and respond from the heart instead of from behind the barrier of a defensive mind.

You want to know what I'm feeling behind what I'm saying, then you will know how to motivate me to grow.

61-75

Building Your Business

Passion equals purpose 94
Maintain recruiting momentum 95
To be serious - be serious! 96
Don't let excitement take over 98
The first things you do and say 99
People are not sponges 100
Relate recruiting to reality 101
Don't scare the new recruits 102
Will your new recruit stay? 104
Success may seem out of reach 105
How are you programmed? 106
You're not in this alone 107
Be prepared to succeed 108
Connecting in your community 109
Multiplication for success 110

Think About 61

Passion equals purpose

It isn't enough to work and hope and dream about things you want to do. To be outstandingly successful you need to have a passion for whatever it is you want to do.

Your passion is what keeps you motivated when things aren't going smoothly.

Your *Why* is what motivates you to be in business, but it is your passion that keeps you there and pushes you to move forward to where you want to go.

You desire something so much, you're willing to do whatever it takes to achieve it.

People have a passion for everything from collecting shoes to building homes to sharing and helping people. Only you know your passion.

Passion drives you when you are tired. It lifts your spirit when you are down and keeps you hopeful when things go wrong. Passion is the over-riding force behind success.

Passion gives you purpose and propels you forward.

Think About 62

Maintain recruiting momentum

Do you lead a busy life and sometimes have difficulty allotting specific time to recruit?

Maintaining momentum is the secret of successful recruiting. It prevents having to constantly gear-up and *re-start* your business. Have you built recruiting momentum, and are you maintaining it?

You can maintain momentum by looking forward. Project your income goal. Compare the time requirements with the time you are willing to invest. Are you being realistic? If necessary, add time or reduce goals to take care of unexpected downtime.

Plan things to help you stay on track. Who can you work with to share what's happening, to talk about ThinkAbout ideas, and to team up to take business building actions together?

Ask yourself what might interfere with your goals and schedule. Allow for holidays, family time, and unforeseen circumstances. To maintain your personal momentum, recruit extra people now for the times you won't be able to recruit later.

Reach for a *stretch goal* to help meet your real goal.

Think About 63

To be serious — be serious!

When you have the determination to decide you want your own business over a job, you deserve to be applauded and you deserve support. But if the decision is a whim, realize to go somewhere you have to get serious.

When you look for, and reach out to, potential recruits who could help you leverage your time and increase your income, you are showing you are serious about growing your business.

If you are serious about succeeding, reaching out will not be something you do half-heartedly and infrequently.

When you are serious about succeeding, one of the first things to learn is that you can achieve your objectives much quicker when you are not working alone.

Recruiting skills can be learned but realize you already know how to share all kinds of news and information.

Have you ever told anyone you've found a good boutique, smart financial advisor, funny movie, or an exciting book? You know how to share good news, capitalize on it! Recruit!

Activator 63

WRITE

Make a list of everything you can think of that you have ever recommended someone do, try, buy, test, see, read or visit.

SELF-EVALUATION

If your list is long, congratulations! If it is short, ask yourself why you don't do more sharing? Do you trust your judgment? Doesn't it feel good to share good news about something you found that was fun, interesting or helpful?

ROLE-PLAY

Pair off with someone and think of something you have read, seen, or done that is interesting, fun, exciting, or worthwhile. Tell the other person about it. Have them do the same to you. Now talk about your feelings. Analyze how doing this made you feel and then talk about how sharing good news relates to recruiting.

PEER OR GROUP DISCUSSION

Most people like to hear about what other people enjoy! Why? Is it presumptuous or generous to share feelings about something you feel is worthwhile? Why do you think some people seldom recommend anything? If you find it difficult to make recommendations, talk about some of the reasons and how to overcome them as a start towards developing the habit of recruiting.

Think About 64

Don't let excitement take over

Signing up a new recruit is a wonderful feeling. Don't allow your excitement to override your very real responsibility.

Never let the joy of finding someone with real potential and a strong interest in doing the business blind you to the fact that this person's fate is initially in your hands.

Your business is easier to do quickly, rather than slowly. The speed at which a new person gets started is almost always an indicator of how far they will go.

Never leave a brand new recruit without setting some realistic goals for first week, first month or months.

Assign activities so they have a specific plan with specific actions to start their business. Set your next date to connect, then prepare a work and follow up schedule.

Make a genuine commitment to match their energy.

Do whatever you can to help make sure that your new recruits get their first check in their hands quickly.

You want it to feel like their birthday or Santa Claus coming early.

Think About 65

The first things you do and say

When you first talk to any person about your product, service or business, you could be talking with a potential recruit. This is where the training and motivation begins.

Far in advance of the person's decision to be recruited, you serve as a role model.

When the time comes to recruit and motivate others, your initial behavior will be long remembered.

What you said, what you did, what you asked, and what you promised will be recalled. And your role-modeling will be repeated again and again.

Ask yourself if your approach and communication style is good enough to be imitated, because it will be!

Your potential recruit's first impression is where your influence and responsibility to them begins.

It can impact your recruit's success and set them up for success, for growth and retention (or it can set them up with bad habits).

Think About 66

People are not sponges

If our minds were like sponges or funnels, it'd be easy to teach people to recruit. But few people *get* all of what they hear the first time they hear it. Reinforcement is a must!

What you need to teach is the importance of learning from and duplicating the successful people in your business. Notice how they listen to the same ideas and lessons over and over. Do you know why?

If you listen to something and take just 10 seconds to relate to what you've heard, in those few seconds you have lost hearing the full thought of whatever comes next.

You won't get the full effect of any thought until you have heard it completely from beginning to end.

So make it a habit to read, review, and listen carefully.

There aren't dumb questions and there aren't poor learners unless it's those who do not listen effectively. Listen, repeat, practice then listen again and practice some more.

Think About 67

Relate recruiting to reality

There are some people who think of recruiting in military terms. It's as if they see recruiting as going out to sign up people ready to go to battle.

In your situation there is no battle. Instead, there is a gift of independence, growth, and a happier and easier future.

Recruiting is selecting someone special to whom you want to offer an opportunity to find peace of mind from the pressure of financial insecurity.

You're offering an opportunity to have extra money and to feel a new, growing sense of achievement.

You're showing people how to be in a position to help themselves and others earn rewards and recognition.

The essence of the word "select" is choosing from among many. How can that be anything but a very nice, memorable, and meaningful compliment?

Think About 68

Don't scare the new recruits

Constant talk about the importance of recruiting can be overwhelming to a newcomer to the business.

In the beginning new people are still unsure about how many prospects are out there.

And even if they sense there are a lot of prospects out there, they don't want to risk losing their potential customers or clients.

Ask the doubters if they know the population of their city and surrounding area.

If the existing team cannot sell and service all these prospects (they can't) you can count on the fact more recruiting help is needed.

Actually, the more people selling and talking about what you offer, the easier it will be to recruit.

It's also easier for everyone to do well selling if more people know about the good image of your company.

Activator 68

WRITE

Pretend someone in a far-away city said all the talk about recruiting bothers her. She's afraid if there are too many people selling in her area, there won't be enough customers for everyone. Write a friendly, warm, motivating letter. Put the letter aside for a few days. Then read it as if you were the recipient.

SELF-EVALUATION

Ask yourself if what you wrote would be enough to convince you of customer potential and the big need for more new recruits in the area. What could be added? Or asked? Do you have any doubts about how convinced you are? Are you willing to reveal them to your Leader so you can be convinced? Certainly you don't believe you can motivate someone else to recruit if your own belief level is low.

PEER OR GROUP DISCUSSION

ASK why do businesses usually grow in direct proportion to the number of people telling others the benefits of what they do? **DISCUSS** how recruiting doesn't have to be learned. It is a natural expression of enthusiasm.

DISCUSS using company materials to tell the company story. **ASK** when and how you begin a recruit's training? If you have actual statistics about your company's market share, show them as examples of potential opportunity.

Think About 69

Will your new recruit stay?

What did you promise? Did you paint things as all blue skies, so disappointment was inevitable if things did not go perfectly?

Right up front, did you explain about the law of averages and why there is no need to feel down or discouraged? Did you talk about why even a *No* has value?

What about the specific promises you made about what to expect concerning training and your support?

Do you keep close tabs on what happens to new recruits, or do they just became a notch on your recruiting belt?

Whether recruits stay or not is a result of you doing what is simple to duplicate, and showing them exactly how to do it, and how to teach others to do it, too.

Just like the 3 Rs in school, your business has 3 Rs. They stand for Recruit (begin), Reinforce (train), and Retain (grow together).

Practice them and then share them with everyone on your team.

Think About 70

Success may seem out of reach

When your potential recruit is looking at teaching, acting, speaking, or selling as things they could never do, recognize there may be a communication barrier.

It's true; most recruits will probably not do these things as well as their Leaders and well-experienced sellers.

What people often fail to see is what practice, exposure, need, desire, intent and satisfaction can contribute to making them much more skilled than they'd ever imagined. Do you know anyone this happened to?

There are many public speakers and famous stars that panic with fear before performances. They're stars, and stay stars, even though they are frightened of not being good enough.

That is why they always try harder!

To be successful is a matter of realizing that the things you thought you could never do, you will do well, simply because you keep trying and practicing.

Most importantly, you care. That's where success starts.

Think About 71

How are you programmed?

Behavioral scientists and psychologists talk a lot about the ways we are mentally programmed to think, feel and act.

What they're talking about is what mothers always have known by instinct.

Remember the little train that said, "I think I can! I think I can!" That's programming a positive attitude.

When you say you "aren't having any luck recruiting," you're programming yourself for poor luck.

When you say, "Everyone's too involved and busy," you are programming yourself to miss the many recruiting opportunities all around you.

You'll begin to create what you want when you program yourself in a new way. Tell yourself, "I attract people who want what I have to offer," or "I meet new people every day to share information about my business."

And then, before you know it, you are successful, and with great delight, you realize you created your success with your positive thoughts and actions.

Persistence always pays off.

Think About 72

You're not in this alone

One of the most wonderful aspects of being in Direct Sales is that you have people in your own company ready to support you as you learn and build your business. There are good people who started just like you did, developed their skills and talents and succeeded beyond their wildest imaginations. Many are eager to share what they learned along the way to help you accelerate your success and could become your mentor.

A good place to find a mentor is in your recruiter or upline Leader. If this is not possible because of distance or some other reason, seek out mentors in the industry. People in Direct Sales are often willing to collaborate. There are organizations like the Direct Selling Women's Alliance (DSWA), with chapters in many states that offer monthly sharing sessions and are not company specific or affiliated.

Also take advantage of the tools your company offers you such as webinars and conference calls. Seek out successful Leaders at company events and ask them questions about their path to the top. Seek out the people that are already where you want to go and learn from them.

Once you succeed, you will have the opportunity to give back to others in the same way. You become a mentor to them, completing the circle of success.

Think About 73

Be prepared to succeed

When you start a Direct Sales business, it's important to put systems and tools in place to grow consistently.

Initially, you need basic things like a PDA or planner for appointments, a business bank account, a stamp or labels with your contact information, and business cards. You'll want a basic filing system for the paperwork you handle like sales slips, contracts or agreements, and leads for customers, potential recruits and the members of your team. A few expandable files will get you started nicely. A computer is a big asset; if you don't have one, many of the tablets on the market have basic functions like e-mail and internet access. You can also go to the library.

If you work for a company with a good back office in their computer system, a lot of tracking and details will be available for you and your team to stay on pace for monthly targets, bonuses and contests.

It is helpful to set up an area within your home to contain your business, and keep everything together in one place. Even if you live in an apartment, find a corner where you can put a desk, even a covered table will do. You can hide boxes and kits under the table so your business doesn't spill over into your living area.

It's simpler to focus on growing your business when you are organized from the start.

Think About 74

Connecting in your community

It is highly likely that you can build your business anywhere you choose with a computer and the myriad of electronic communications and social media options available today.

One of the most convenient and cost effective places to build business is still your local area, from your neighborhood, to your town, and then in a 30 minute radius of where you live. There are many opportunities to develop strong relationships in your community and the surrounding area.

There is great power in networking meetings and involvement in community groups. When you join a group, select one that matches your interests, not just a place to build business. Go beyond attending meetings, get on the board or a committee so you interact with people on a deeper level.

Plan to stay with a group for at least a year. It takes time to build trust and to really get to know the members.

When you participate, you build a fine reputation for who you are, not just what you do. It's amazing what you can convey when you meet people face to face and you spend time together working for a common interest. Business and referrals follow as you build relationships.

Multiplication for success

The arithmetic of this business is simple and logical. Understanding it is great motivation for income growth.

Addition is YOU + 1 + 1 + 1. Not everyone signs on for life so totals can change making addition alone a slow way to meet your promotion and financial objectives.

A key secret to success is duplication by multiplication.

Multiplication is YOU + 1+ 1+ 1 and some ambitious recruits also focused on adding 1+1+ 1. Visualize that in your mind. Thanks to math it's simple to project $$$.

It's easy to see isn't it? With your team working with you multiplying each month, growth has no limits except what you set in terms of time investment. You plus your team working with their teams all doing the same activities creates synergy, which makes work fun and rewarding on many levels. Think shared goals and new lifetime friends! You are in the business of building people. Promotions increase income; they are a cause for celebration and wonderful recognition.

Think 3! Recruit – Reinforce - Retain. Imagine you start with 3 people on your team adding 3 recruits like you do each month. 4 recruiters x 3 recruits = 12 new team recruits. Isn't multiplication becoming your favorite type of math?

76 - 86

Talking to Yourself

A hangover from childhood 112
There's joy and disappointment 113
Some things are easy 114
The magic of knowing your numbers 116
Sometimes "No" is a gift 117
Get out of your comfort zone 118
You are wise! 119
Be prepared for resistance 120
Tomorrow doesn't always come 121
A story about a farmer 122
What happened to yesterday? 124

Think About 76

A hangover from childhood

Remember when you were a child how you felt about the *have-to-dos* the adults demanded?

When it was school time, we wanted to play. When it was summertime we missed school activities and we missed doing things with our school friends.

When we grew up, too many of us had established a pattern of thinking that quite often *must-do* activities were a bore.

When we hear recruiting is a *must-do,* we rebel, or find it is difficult to get started with enthusiasm.

Is recruiting like that for you? Do questions like these bother you? "Have you done any recruiting?" "Did you sign them up?"or "What happened?"

If recruiting feels like a chore instead of a rewarding positive experience, this is the time to change old thinking patterns and recruit joyfully. Recruiting brings personal growth to enrich your life!

There's joy and disappointment

You've often heard that nothing is all black or all white, there's always something in between.

Recruiting is like that, some good stuff, some not so good stuff. What needs to stay good is your attitude.

When you find and sign up an ambitious new recruit, it will never cease to be a joy. If the new recruit doesn't succeed or doesn't stay, it may be a disappointment.

It is also reality. Frequently, they don't keep on believing that they have potential. And belief is everything.

That's why it's critical you always do two things to improve the chances of long-term retention.

1. Make certain your new recruit sees success and gets a commission check as soon as possible.
2. Hang in there. In person or by phone, be there to support your willing and trainable new recruits over the first hurdles until their feet are firmly planted on the road to success.

Show your joy. It's contagious!

Think About 78

Some things are easy

There are things we do so regularly we never even think about doing them because they are so easy to do.

Setting the alarm and getting up.

Brushing our teeth and combing our hair.

It's the new things we're asked to remember, things that are out of our usual pattern such as recruiting, that we tend to overlook or forget to do every day.

So it's a good idea to make recruiting a habit to make sure you don't ever let recruiting become a *sometime* activity.

Recruit naturally and consistently. Be aware and always ready to meet a prospective customer or business builder.

Recruit whenever and wherever you meet new people. Make it a habit to be on the lookout for people to recruit! They are out there! Some are literally *waiting* for you.

Activator 78

WRITE

List some of the things that you do as a habit, meaning that you just do them. You don't have to take time to think consciously; "This is what I am going to do and this is how I will do it".

SELF-ANALYSIS

How did you develop your everyday habits? Assume that you want to develop a new habit, and you feel very strongly about it. What will you do to make doing something new (or doing something differently) a positive new habit?

TALK ABOUT

You are a Leader who is highly motivated to teach your people how to develop the habit of recruiting. What will your strategy be for doing this? What are some of the things you will tell new recruits to try? How will you evaluate what happens?

PEER AND GROUP DISCUSSION

ASK yourself when it comes to things related to recruiting, what do you do habitually? You do it so naturally you never have to think about doing it. What kinds of new recruiting habits would you like to develop? Do you have any ideas about how to be sure a particular recruiting activity becomes a habit? Did you know if you do anything for thirty days in a row you will develop a new habit? Have you ever tried this? What happened?

Think About 79

The magic of knowing your numbers

Learn how numbers can help you motivate yourself!

Keep score of approaches so you know exactly how many people to talk to in order to get one recruiting appointment.

How many people on average must hear about your business opportunity to get a *Yes* response to sign a new recruit?

How many new recruits do you need to add to develop a team builder or new Leader?

Recruiting approaches and interview time are convincing time, and training time is team building time.

Like magic, double the value of your time by having local new team members observe you so you are training live.

Know and understand your compensation plan so you can explain how recruiting can add to and multiply your growing income.

Keep track of where you are right now and also know where you want to be one year and five years from now.

Let the magic of knowing your numbers motivate you!

Think About 80

Sometimes "No" is a gift

After you review your first list of contacts with your mentor you'll discuss the recruiting approaches and the best thing to say to people on your warm list.

When you try it, it doesn't always work. Maybe it was the wrong approach or time. Perhaps, you did not reflect a positive attitude and enthusiasm about what you do. Whatever, the reason, the *No* hurt. It shouldn't. Statistically, it is just one step closer to *Yes*!

When you talk about what happened, it becomes a learning experience. When you have been working in the business longer you might sometimes consider *No* a blessing.

Your job is not to just add new recruits to your roster. You don't have to convince somebody to do something that just doesn't suit them or fit their objective or personality, or that might conflict with yours.

Sometimes a *No* can be a gift. Every person that says *No* has a friend, relative, neighbor or coworker, who wouldn't say *No*. So you have been gifted with a second chance to ask for referrals.

Say, "Now that you know more about my business, do you know someone who might be interested in hearing about making money alongside their life? I really need help in this neighborhood." They might change their mind.

Think About 81

Get out of your comfort zone

Like a little kid dragging around a blanket for a feeling of security, are you dragging around some old fears?

Think of the butterfly, so ugly as it's growing and so lovely when it breaks out of its cocoon and flies on its own.

If you are limiting yourself to people you know, or who know you or who you meet in structured situations, you may be tying yourself to the temporary security of only the first step to success.

Like the butterfly there is a *world of adventure* out there waiting for you to fly out to it.

When you have opportunities to talk to strangers, realize that hearing a compliment from you could not only change their mood, but in some cases it might even change their life.

If you're too comfortable in your cocoon, you are denying yourself the joy of flying!

Think About 82

You are wise!

You have chosen security in a time of up and down economic conditions and predictions. Direct Sales is a growing opportunity because people want to enhance their skills. They are willing to fill needs and share freely with others. Be proud because you are recruiting others into this entrepreneurial industry.

You had the guts to reach out to do something to increase your income and use your natural skills. Building your own business is an investment in your future.

You recognize the limitations of today's job market and dependence on others. You have vision to see a future where you are in control

You are a realist. You know that you get out of your business what you put into it. Success is waiting for you to claim it. You are wise. You recognize your business is a way to leverage your time. You are building a team to generate income with you.

You are secure. You have no need to fear downsizing, layoffs, or mergers. You can increase your effort and your income. You enjoy freedom as an independent entrepreneur. You are a good role model. People learn from you what schools didn't teach; to have dreams and goals and how to achieve them.

Think About 83

Be prepared for resistance

When you are in the midst of an approach, presentation or interview, sometimes prospects start nodding their head *Yes* almost from the beginning. Those people are all ears and waiting for your message.

That's very nice if it happens, but do not expect it.

More often than not, you will face doubts, maybe fears, certainly skepticism, and always WIIFM. In other words, your prospect is wondering, "What's in it for me?"

If you haven't built WIIFM into what you share, you don't deserve a *Yes*. You'll only get one by accident.

There's really nothing to object to about what you do, or you wouldn't be doing it. But it's only natural that for self-protection or desire to know more, you may get some resistance.

Expect resistance and understand it.

Learn what to say when someone resists so that you can help them understand the personal benefits of your offer.

Learn to turn their resistance into the reason that your business opportunity is just right for them.

Think About 84

Tomorrow doesn't always come

Most people have good intentions. I'm sure you believe that. But what happens to those good intentions in real life scenarios? Somehow, something breaks down between that good intention and what really happens. Often the excuse is; "I'm sorry, I just forgot."

The people on the receiving end of that message surely get the idea they are not high on your list of priorities. So chances are they'll change your name position on theirs.

Procrastination is painful to those who have it and those who are affected by it. It contributes to failure in schools, relationships, marriages, politics and careers. However, some people do get over it. If you have it, chances are that you can too.

You may not have the same focus that the "always on time never late for anything people" have built into them. You don't want to fail. Realize you're in big trouble then create a plan and begin to build good habits.

Find someone who will partner with you and talk with you for 30 days in a row to help you get back on track. Establish a daily check-in call to report your progress. They agree to call you if you miss the check-in time, to see if you did what you planned. Today, you can run your life with your cell phone or a planner APP. There are paid services and people who can remind you of things. If you need help, be willing to pay for it.

Think About 85

A story about a farmer

There was once was a farmer who dreamed for years about mining and finding diamonds instead of dealing with all the planting and plowing and weather problems of farming.

He saved and saved and denied himself and his family all of the pleasures in life.

Finally, the time came to sell his farm and he set out for foreign lands where he felt diamonds were waiting to be discovered.

He didn't discover a single diamond. He squandered all of his money and in the end he committed suicide in total despair.

However, the family who bought his farm found valuable diamonds glistening in the stream, right on the farmer's old property. The farm actually became the biggest diamond mine ever discovered.

When you are going off in all directions seeking new recruits, remember this story and ask yourself if you have sought out potential right where you live.

There are probably diamonds in the rough that can be polished into good recruits right in your own backyard.

Don't overlook the familiar just because it doesn't seem possible that finding new recruits could be so easy and so convenient.

Activator 85

TALK ABOUT

Did you ever have a recruit right under your nose and someone else recruited them? If this happened to you, how would you feel? Did you ever go far away from home to find a recruit, and then discovered one next door or right in the neighborhood?

SELF-EVALUATION

Some people have a "grass is greener" complex. Wherever these people are, no matter how lucky they are, they look at the other side of the fence and think things would be better if that's where they were. Do you ever feel like this? Why?

Is feeling like this a way to distract you from having to do something? Is it a way for you to avoid responsibility or success? Or do you honestly not realize you've developed a "grass is greener" attitude? If you feel you do have this kind of attitude, who will you ask to help you change and defeat it?

PEER AND GROUP DISCUSSION

ASK why and how the diamond story relates to recruiting? Do you know of any situation that has happened to you or someone else that reminds you of the farmer?

DISCUSS whether a diamond glows, shines and sparkles as soon as it is discovered? What has to be done to a rough diamond that relates to your responsibility to the new recruits? If you were thinking about recruits as diamonds, how many do you want to find? How soon? And where do you intend to do your mining? What is the easiest or most unusual recruiting example you've ever heard someone talk about?

Think About 86

What happened to yesterday?

That's the day you were going to do it all, and do it right, and not let yourself to be distracted.

It didn't happen. Now, today, you're having a hard time getting started because you're bogged down with regrets.

The secret of success is to eliminate potential regrets.

Today will be tomorrow's yesterday, so plan now to feel good about your accomplishments.

You own a precious gift that no one can give you; the ability to make the decisions as to how you spend what will be your yesterdays.

Every night ask yourself just two questions:

"What did I do today to make someone happy?" "What did I do today to move me toward achieving my dreams and goals?"

Make sure you go to bed with happy answers so you will have no regrets about missed opportunities.

The Importance of Recruiting Appointments

Recruiting appointments, this is where your business explodes by consistently approaching people to connect. It's one of the key pieces in building your business. But you can't make an approach without someone to talk to, right? You know better than that.

While it is true, you ***do*** need someone to talk to; in reality, there is always someone to connect with if you are willing to reach out. Regardless of what product or service you offer, there are probably hundreds of people who would commit to being a shopper, a member, a host, or a recruit if they only knew about your product and company. Approaching people is a marketing strategy where you identify who you are and what you do to create interest and to connect with the people with whom you'd like an appointment to talk to about your business.

If you hesitate to reach out, re-read the ThinkAbouts and Activators for actions to take to make connections. When you reach out to help others, there is a really nice by-product; helping yourself! You are in business, stay in it and build it.

Out of inventory - out of business

If you own a store and run out of inventory, you would be out of business, right? In this business your inventory is names. If you have not collected those names, or have become complacent or over-confident, believing you did not need an inventory of contacts to connect with, you are essentially out of business. Make prospecting fun, make it a daily game. Try it and see.

As you collect new names you can role model how to do this for your team. Everyone you work with should be aware that only a tiny percentage of the population you meet, even if you represent a billion-dollar company, know anything about what you offer. There are many good prospects wherever you go. Knowing this is like having diamonds in your own backyard. However, if you don't seek them out, they will stay buried like a treasure for someone else to find. Prove it to yourself by finding them.

What are you doing weekly to show your team that prospecting is simply reaching out to find someone to help? An approach is simply reaching out in different ways to get a date to talk, or to get a referral.

Reaching out to share something good is the simple part of the business. Initially, it may seem difficult, when you do it right and often, it will quickly become the most rewarding.

Friends you haven't met yet

Your mother or grandmother probably told you never to talk to strangers. That was good advice when you were a child. You are now an adult. I learned a long time ago that, "a stranger is just a friend you haven't met yet." This philosophy has allowed me to develop friendships with dozens, even hundreds, of people that I would have never met without sharing the business opportunity.

Whenever you reach out to a stranger, if only to give them a compliment and make them feel good, it hurts no one and it just might benefit both of you. Any conversation, anywhere, may offer a clue that this might be a prospect or someone you could help. As an additional benefit, if you always ask for referrals, you are bound to hear, "What about me?" from some of the people you approach.

Start to build your name inventory by listing the 100 people who might come to your birthday party, your college graduation, your wedding or your child's baptism. Then think about which approach category they might fit into from the categories in the next section.

Approaching new people is essential for long term business success and increasing your income. We share our system to help you increase your results in getting appointments so your success can significantly exceed the average.

We encourage you to be the kind of person that people like to associate with and spend time with in life or in business. Be neat, clean, well prepared and happy. Be enthusiastic about your product and your business opportunity.

You don't have to be outgoing or effervescent, or anything other than yourself. It is your interest in the other person and the depth of your belief and willingness to talk with them that counts.

Every time you approach someone to get a date to talk about your business there is one overall quality that will help you get results: genuine sincerity.

Be prepared and organized about scheduling time and appointments. Be sure to leave enough time between appointments to stay on schedule and to arrive on time for the next one.

Many successful people use checklists as part of their essential organization system, to stay on top of what needs to be done. If you operate without a system, it will work against you and limit your effectiveness. If you don't have a system now, ask successful people in your company what they do or create one that fits your personal style.

Making an approach is a lot different than giving a presentation and the two should never be confused. The purpose of an approach is simple; to make a date to give a presentation. The way you build curiosity or create a sense of benefits without giving details is the key to achieving a high ratio of success on your approach scorecard. The purpose of a presentation is to deliver the full business story, opportunity, and compensation information. It should be designed to get a commitment, a *Yes*!

Our system for designing an effective approach involves five elements that take you from the beginning to the end. We call it the "The ION APPROACH SYSTEM" because this is a system filled with energy and the five steps all end with an ION.

The steps are: Communication – Clarification – Simplification – Amplification and Examination. Let's look at each one.

Communication

After consistent practice you'll find making an approach becomes the easiest thing you have to do. It should be just like saying, "Hello." More often than not, you are saying hello to a stranger. To get to the point where you are really effective making a connection quickly, you need a lot of practice. Until you're comfortable you don't want to ad-lib anything this important.

Do what top show business professionals do. They rehearse and then they rehearse some more and they do it in front of a mirror. Look at the various approach appeals we have given you and role play in front of a mirror. Don't be shy!

Clarification

Whether you are talking to a stranger or a friend you want this to be a brief short contact. You want to make it very clear up front that the purpose of this brief contact is to set up a date to talk to them in detail about something you believe could change their life or fill a specific need that you are aware of in their life.

The structuring of this situation is important. You do not want it to turn into a discussion or to talk too much. This is a fleeting contact with two goals: 1. To get a *Yes* to talk, and 2. To get a *date* for a presentation or interview.

Simplification

One of the most important rules of communication is to take the time to structure, to prepare a sequence for what you are going to say. When you are structuring, be sure to come from the vantage point of the person with whom you are speaking.

If you say, "you're excited," that's not from the vantage point of the other person. Try saying "I know you are going to be excited when you hear about ___."

Select a question, or a statement, for your *opener*.

There are multiple reasons they should consider meeting with you. It is your responsibility to play up the advantages for them and to do it in the time it takes to watch a 30 second TV commercial or less. If your message is more than 80 words, it is probably too long. Say as much as you can in the shortest amount of time.

Amplification

When you have a strong message to share, keep sharing it again and again. Leverage your time and double your exposure. Build trust up front, by asking, "Why don't you ask someone whose judgment you respect to join us?" More often than not, the extra person is another strong prospect and you end up with two new team members, instead of just one.

Examination

How often have you taken the time right after an approach to evaluate what happened and why? Was what you said and did with your prospect as good as it should have been? How could you improve before the next one?

Make time to reflect on your efforts and results and assess your effectiveness. If your ratio of *No* to *Yes* is too high; you need to analyze what you are saying and doing. Use a legal pad and write out what is working for you, what is not working for you, and what you need to do differently to increase your results.

Ask for help from your Leader or mentor if needed. The beauty of this type of business is that there is always someone nearby, just a call or text away, to offer support or ideas. We can't see ourselves as others do, so our self-improvement efforts may not work effectively without help from someone else. G. Sherle is well known for saying, "When in doubt, reach out!"

When you reach out in this business it's like giving a gift. You're showing one of the best qualities of a Leader. You're showing you are open and confident enough to trust and respect the opinions and input of others. Both of you will be enriched, you with improved skills for increasing results, and the other person with the good feeling that they were able to support your growth.

Scheduling appointments effectively

Always get a confirmed date and time for an appointment rather than a *maybe*. It's better to call back and schedule it at another time that you can confirm or it may just cancel.

It's best to schedule appointments with business people in their office, only if they promise to give you their uninterrupted attention for XX minutes. Otherwise suggest an alternative time and place to meet. Say something like; "We could meet at a coffee shop, restaurant or even the lobby of a hotel near where you work or live. I could come to your home or you could come to my home office. Which is most convenient for you?"

If prospects say they are too busy to meet, ask if they take a lunch break then suggest you meet and they can eat while you talk.

Remember your objective in approaching someone is simply to get a date and time for an appointment. You want to create enough curiosity to get the date but not to tell so much they can decide they are not interested in spending the time to hear more.

70 Approaches that Work!

Just as there is a wide variety of people to approach who might be interested in your business, or know someone to recommend, there are a wide variety of approaches. Let's look at several now.

Curiosity

- Are you with NOC (Name of company) yet? (This assumes they will be).
- Can you imagine what it would be like if you could ____?
- Do you know in only a few hours a week you could ____?
- I love it that I can work from home and get out of debt.

Compliment

- I have a hunch you would be terrific doing what I do. Let's have coffee so I can tell you about it.
- Do you know that a friendly smile like yours is worth money?
- Watching you, I have a feeling you are just the kind of person I'm looking for. Could we meet and see if you could be even half as excited as I am about my new found financial freedom working alongside of my busy life?

Imperative

- There is something I just have to show you ASAP!
- Are you free Tuesday or Thursday evening so I could stop by? Or would Saturday morning be better?
- (Name), I need to see you. I've found something, and I have no idea if you'd be interested, but I know you know people who I could help. I need your advice. Could we meet either ___ or___?
- (Name) we have got to talk ASAP. I found something that we should do together to add to our income even though we're so short on time.
- We have got to get together this week. This can't wait!

Direct

- (Name), if I could show you something that makes total sense and could be done in a few hours a week, would you be interested in adding to your monthly income?
- Who do you know who…(ad lib personal appeal such as, needs money, needs a part time job, enjoys helping others, has a great personality, fun to be around?)
- Assuming you are like most of us, would you like to have a second income if it didn't interfere with your busy life or career? How about a new ____? (car, home, travel etc.)
- (Name), would you like to be able to stay home and have other people making money for themselves and for you at the same time? If you could do this without interfering at all with your current job or responsibilities, would you be interested?

Clue Generated

- (Name), I've an idea that can help you solve that problem.
- I'm very excited. I have an idea to help you with ____. We need to talk! How about ___ or ___?
- I know several people who were facing the same challenge. They've found a great solution, when can we talk?

Research

- I'm looking for people who would like a second income without having to take a second job—who do you know who is worried about money or downsizing?
- Who do you know who is facing sudden extra expenses, or is interested in building financial security?
- (Act like a "head hunter") Is this (Name)? I understand you are the manager of (name of store). Do you have about 90 seconds to talk right now?
- This is (Your Name) with NOC and we're expanding in your area. I understand you know lots of people, I'm wondering if you know anyone who would like an extra $XXX to $XXXX per month without interfering with their regular job?

- Do you know anyone who isn't happy in their job but needs the paycheck and might like to "job test" something new without having to leave where they're working currently?

Group

- I'm inviting some of my friends over to hear about what I've found that would be fun to do together. We can make extra money, too. Can you stop by around seven on Tuesday?
- I've found the most wonderful group of people who are showing me how to have fun making extra money and I really want my friends to know what I'm doing. We don't see each other enough; can you come by at seven on Tuesday night? Trust me. This is really interesting.

Financial

- Have you noticed that prices keep going up? I wonder if you'd be interested in a way to have extra money without getting a new or second job.
- Who do you know who is worried about job security?
- (When you get a compliment on something new you are wearing) Thank you. I got it with my (NOC) check. You've just got to hear about what I'm doing. I am having a blast!

Business

- I know you're doing very well in your business (or profession), but if there were an opportunity that you could fit in alongside of it, to give you a very generous increase in income, would you be interested in hearing about it?
- Are you sick of being in the rat race, (or of working for someone else), yet?
- If my partner and I could show you how you could have a XXXXX figure extra income within a few years would you look at it if there is no (or low) investment?
- I'm looking for some new partners who would like to make extra income on the side with no (or low) investment. When can we get together so I can share it with you?
- I've always respected you as a business person, and I just discovered something with no (or low) investment that looks

like a winner. I'd like you to take a look at it and give me your opinion. Do you have about XX minutes?

Time

- I know how busy you are, but there is something I have just got to show/share with you. What would be the best time this week for us to meet for coffee?
- Are you going to be home Tuesday night? Good! I'm going to stop by for about XX minutes. I have something to show you.
- I've got one foot out the door but I wanted to call and see if you are going to be home Tuesday?

Cold call approaches to sales people

- We don't know each other, but I've heard you are doing a great job selling ____, and I know we have something in common. How about coffee this week?
- We both get most of our business from referrals. I'd like to meet you for coffee or I'll buy you lunch - you eat - I'll talk. We can compare notes about how we might help each other. Do you have your schedule handy?

  TIP: *Every time you go shopping, look for excellent salespeople. Most are underpaid. Shop in stores that sell products or services related to what you offer. Stop in stores admitting you're just looking (you are) and start a conversation. Pick a nearby spot for coffee and you can meet several on the same day. Allow plenty of time between appointments and expect some no shows. Be prepared with something to work on or do in between.*

Cold call approach to neighbor

- Hi! This is (Your Name), your neighbor, and although we haven't talked much, I'd like to have coffee with you and tell you about something I've discovered that might interest you. When would be a good time to talk for about XX minutes?

Cold call approach to young mother

- If you are like most of the mothers I know, you'd love to have more quality time with your children, and I know a way that can happen. I'd like to set up a time to tell you about it. How about meeting for coffee for about XX minutes this week?

- If she's not interested –always pay her a compliment and ask for a referral for someone who might like to spend more time with their children, needs money, wants time freedom, etc...

Phone call to someone you met briefly

- Are you interruptible? I hope you remember me. We met briefly at __________and I've been thinking about you. I'd like to tell you about something you can do around the edges of your busy life to make a little, or a lot of money. When would be a good time to talk today or tomorrow?
- You may not remember me, but I remember thinking that I ought to talk to you because_____ (insert compliment).

Approaching a stranger

- Are you free for a few minutes? You live in an area where I need ambitious moms who don't want a full time job. I can show them how they can increase their monthly income and have fun doing it. Do you know anyone I should talk to? Someone who likes to help people and would like to earn extra money or have more flexible work hours?
- You live in an area where I need to find some moms who would like to "job test" a new career while still employed, that will allow them to stay home with their children, and make more money than they ever anticipated they could.
- I help people "job test" a part-time career in a way that won't interfere with regular job.
- I owe you an apology. Do you have a minute to talk? This is (Your Name) and someone gave me your name, and I've been carrying it around a while because I can't remember why I was supposed to call you. Would you be interested in _____?
- If you noticed me watching you I to want apologize. I just have the strongest hunch you'd enjoy the work I do.
- Is there any chance you'd be open to extra income working at home and in your choice of times? (If no—be sure to ask for referrals and in the process arouse some curiosity.)

Attending events (When you don't have a table)

- Be subtle. With strangers, ask what they've found interesting and why they came to the show. In the process, they will tell you about themselves, listen carefully. Then say, "I know something you'd like to know about. Let's exchange cards; we really shouldn't talk about another opportunity here. I'll call you." (Pin down a good time to call.)

Working a table

- Go to meetings, programs, breakfasts, lunches, and dinners that attract the type of people you are looking for. Don't monopolize the conversation at your table, instead, help get people talking by having everyone tell where they are from or what they do. Collect cards. Put reminder notes on the back of cards to help you when you make a follow up call.

Networking meetings

- Prepare a 10, 30, and 60 second introduction so you have something ready for the amount of time they give you. Here are some examples.

  10 seconds: *Name, business name, catchy tagline that people will ask you about*

  30 seconds: *Name, business name, description of people who will benefit from what you offer*

  60 seconds: *Name, business name, the types of people who would be good referrals for you for sales and as team members*

  Try preparing many versions so you always have alternatives.

The power of referrals

- This is one of the very best ways to get good new leads to call and it is way too often overlooked or forgotten. Keep in mind that people like to be asked for advice and many people welcome the opportunity to be of service to others. Don't hesitate to ask for advice from successful people.

- (Name) I am building my own business and realize you have done well in the business world. When could we talk so I can share what I do and see if you can direct me to some people that may want to hear about it?

(After an appointment, when no interest is shown)

- Now that you know more about my company and services, is there anyone that you know that could benefit from hearing about this opportunity?
- (Name), since you are not interested in this opportunity, can you give me the names of three people in the area that might be looking for more income or a business that fits around the rest of their life?
- If you make an approach or a presentation, and you don't get a "Yes," at least get referrals by using these three trigger words that get attention. Use this exact question. "Who do you know who'd **appreciate** being **alerted** to the **opportunity** to _____ (your offer)?"
- If you want to approach people obliquely, ask for referrals as your reason for talking to them.
- Think of neighborhood business owners who are good with people such as the local dry cleaner or instant print store owner. Ask who they know who might be interested in _____. Be sure they know that you show people how to ____ so they can recommend that you get together with them to talk.
- If the product or service you offer represents, or is related to, a certain field (health, nutrition, beauty, accessorizing, hair care, shopping, decorating, etc.) ask about people they know in related services as referrals.
- To get an opportunity to make an approach and schedule a time to talk, you have to generate interest. The two best ways to do that are to say something that will make them curious or to give them a sense of personal benefit.
- To establish a quick relationship so that people trust you, you have to be open and honest in the way you lead up to the approach statement or question.
- Always remember the dual objective is: 1. To help the prospect like you so you can get a firm appointment to talk with them, and 2. To build trust in you and your company.

Time to talk - not time for a mini presentation

- For prospects who want answers to questions up front you can say: "If I had a beautiful painting, would you want me to show a tiny piece and expect you to see the whole beautiful picture with all its detail? It'll only take XX minutes to share the information with you."
- Instead of making statements about what you have to offer, why not ask questions which will help define their hot button. What gets them excited?
- If they ask to see a website instead of meeting with you, simply say something like this, "We have an excellent website. I want to take you there ***but,*** this is the only time you'll ever be brand new so I'd like to take you through it personally because I know that will help you the most."

  TIP: *Many companies have marketing websites or online information for prospects to view. Whenever possible, go to the website with your prospect, in person or on the phone, and then answer questions immediately following the presentation and ask for a decision to join your team and to get started right now.*
- If you cannot view the material with them, ask them to call you as soon as they have viewed it.
- If you have a company program to view online and are sending the link to many people, ask for a call, text or e-mail with their thoughts or comments after the viewing to enter them into a weekly drawing. This cues you to follow up right away with the people who were interested or curious enough to view the information.
- Some prospects will tell you right away they absolutely aren't interested because they or someone they know has been disappointed or lost money in one of those "home business things." Respond quickly saying, "I'm really sorry to hear that, but I have to admit that showing my opportunity to you will be a whole lot easier because you will immediately understand the differences and know how valid and good this opportunity is, let's talk."

There you have it. Seventy different ways to connect with people to get an appointment to share your business opportunity. The more people you reach out to, the better your results will be.

It's totally up to you how much time you invest in your business. If you don't invest consistently, there will be a price to pay. On a week that you need extra money you may not meet the people who will help you meet your goals. The good news is that you can *always* start again.

Work with the law of averages and know what your personal averages are for getting the results you desire. Choose to take your business seriously. Take the time to seek out and talk to long timers, as well as today's most successful Leaders.

People love to be around enthusiastic people. Be enthusiastic! Your interest in other people and the feelings you generate about having something really important to share will win them over. People just want to do business with people who are passionate about what they do!

Remember, be sincere in everything you do. Whether it's a recruiting approach, presenting the story of your company, selling your product, or servicing a customer - sincerity gets results.

Be prepared. Present with joy and contagious confidence. Be proud of your company and share your belief in your opportunity. Watch the best people present, and realize this can be YOU!

Dealing with Resistance

Resistance is normal. It is human nature to hear about something new for the first time and to push back, put up your guard, or to proceed cautiously.

All human beings go through a process to accept a new idea. It is highly likely that what you present to most people regarding starting a business will be a new idea.

The six steps to acceptance

1. Total rejection
2. Partial rejection
3. Partial acceptance
4. Total acceptance
5. Partial assimilation
6. Total assimilation

How it plays out when presenting your opportunity:

(You approach someone for the first time)

1. No thanks, I'm not interested. I could never sell anything.

(After you talk further about their needs and dreams)

2. Really? You think I could do this and make some money?

(You answer questions and offer support)

3. Well, maybe I could give it a try for a couple of months?

(You offer the agreement or to go online with them to fill it out)

4. OK, I'm ready to get started.

(You discuss a date to introduce their new business to friends and family)

5. They schedule a business launch event and start building.

(After some training, they are engaged and building)

6. They talk with people and confidently present the product and opportunity on their own.

Some people get through the whole process in seconds, some people never get through all of the steps.

It's always a good idea to explore and review your company's literature. Chances are high that there's some really helpful information that you don't even know exists about almost every area of your business, but most certainly about dealing with natural resistance.

Did you notice we use the term *natural resistance* instead of the usual sales phrase which is *dealing with objections?* Why? You would not be out there representing your company if there were something *objectionable* involved. What you are dealing with is truly a *natural resistance.* Thinking about it this way makes it easier to handle.

Expect resistance and accept it

To deal with resistance, get comfortable with it, accept it as normal, expect it, learn to handle it and turn it into the reason someone should look at your opportunity. The better you become at dealing with resistance, the stronger you will become at recruiting consistently. An easy resistance to deal with is from people who feel they have no skills. You can make them feel wonderful by showing them they do have *natural skills* that have value. Encourage them to explore this idea. They'll feel so good when they realize what you said is true.

On the other hand, the most difficult resistance to deal with might be "I am looking at something else." Here you need to evaluate their interest in what your company offers and remind them of things that appealed to them. Ask for a chance to compare programs. There is probably something about yours that may have more appeal, or benefit them more, or have a competitive advantage over whatever else they are considering. It's worth exploring the value your offer brings to the table.

Resistance asks for relaxation. Whatever you do, stay positive! Thinking, "Here comes a *No,*" or getting defensive can push your prospect away. The rules are to stay cool, charming, and prepared with logical answers and good common sense. A *No* is not the end of the world. Your attitude is everything! Consider getting a *No* as an opportunity to get more practice. As you know, the best musicians, the best actors, the best communicators never stop practicing and improving their skills. Shouldn't you?

Grandma Sherle on Communication

Long ago, before your time, people talked about beginning education with the three R's. You probably know this meant reading, 'riting and 'rithmetic. Well, we've come a long way. Today babies can sign before they walk. Kids, so tiny they have to sit on pillows, can play their favorite computer games and be involved for hours, which both amazes and alarms us. How could we have known that in our lifetime a computer that filled the room could be replaced by a chip smaller than the tip of your little finger and do hundreds of thousands times more?

In our high tech society it's astounding what 140 characters can do. You can sell millions of dollars of products and bond people together for a cause 140 characters at a time. New technology bombards us daily. It increases the amount of contact, but it doesn't really improve or build relationships.

Look around you. You will see two teenagers on a date and instead of talking to each they are texting. Groups of teens and college kids will carry on separate discussions in the same room without speaking a word. Married people who don't see enough of each other are on a date. He's watching a game on his cell phone and she's calling her girl friend. There are a lot of people around them doing the same thing. In almost every business meeting there is texting going on, often surreptitiously under the table. E-mails, photos, texts and videos are being sent at any time, even when attention should be elsewhere.

Add the distracting visuals and sounds that impact our days, surrounding us wherever we go. People are selling or learning things or playing games to amuse themselves in every waking moment. Google seems to run the world leaving text books and dictionaries and even teachers behind. Asking questions is now high tech. All of this distracts from our relationships. You need to know what's happening and how to make it work for you.

We should assume within 10 years, maybe sooner, it'll be difficult to get people to sit and concentrate on anything. The average person is going to find it harder and harder to focus and avoid distraction.

People will read less and for shorter periods of time. There are some publications that may be exempt, including the Bible and religious books, fiction which is driven by plot, instructional material, motivational books, cookbooks, and some best sellers. Distraction will become a universal problem. This will affect recruiting and every aspect of your personal and business lives. In a world of increased distraction, competition will expand beyond what we are able to imagine today. We need to think about it.

Since the 1990s, when Faith Popcorn first began predicting trends, we think of eras in terms of marketplace needs. We're still in the era where the dominant need is to be *connected*. We are moving into an era where everything is about building and maintaining relationships. We need to know we're not alone. Technology helps us stay connected, but it also presents a whole new set of challenges.

Learning how to connect with people despite increasing distractions and technology-overload are important issues for educators, families, businesses, and people like you, who contribute to a company's growth. As much as possible, we should engage a person's eyes, ears, and mind to keep their attention. One important way to accomplish this is through printed materials that are visually stimulating. Design and layout are often more important than content. After all, if you don't capture *and keep* the reader's attention, the content will never be understood.

As time passes, books will get lighter on words, and heavier on eye-catching graphics. Good communication will likely include dimension, motion, and sound, as evidenced already by the new QR codes accessible on smart phones, or the new Vook - eBooks with implanted videos.

Everyone who wants or needs to communicate anything in writing is going to have to learn to *Communicut* to Communicate. For more information on how to make communication and training simpler, quicker, and more engaging, e-mail Ro at ro@roshales.com.

More Thoughts on Communication

- Remember, the most important rule of communication is to talk only from the other person's vantage point, not from yours. If you are excited about something that's fine, but say, "I think you might be really excited!" Then tell them why.

This is one of the most essential communication rules, and the most neglected.

- There are only four reasons people listen to anything regardless of their age or position. 1) They sense a personal benefit. 2) You've made them curious. 3) They are courteous. 4) They love you. Think about this, age doesn't matter. This rule applies to everyone.
- Never ask anyone if they understood you; the *Yes* or *No* answer will tell you nothing. Instead ask them to tell you what you just told them, to make sure you communicated it clearly.
- When you ask a question and get a response, count silently and slowly in your head 1-2-3 before you respond. You will be surprised how much more information you will absorb.
- Assumption is the single biggest cause of a communication breakdown. Let the person you are speaking with know you are not assuming you know what they think. It's perfectly okay to say, "I know you have some things you need to know to evaluate what I am sharing with you. I will be happy to answer all of your questions so you can make an informed decision."
- In planning what to say, give more consideration to questions you can ask, rather than the statements that you can make.
- Try to be mentally or emotionally connected when communicating with people; until you see what they see or understand what they feel you will not know what they mean.

Communicate to Build Relationships

The people who are good at building relationships don't have any more time than you do. But they know that investing just a little bit of time to make people feel good or special will pay off in the long run. Try it, and chances are high that your customers will start working for you, because they know you care. They'll start giving you more referrals.

Start from day one to build good relationships. The day after someone joins your team is the best day to call to welcome them. Share your excitement to work with and support them. If there is an appropriate compliment, now is the time to give it. And then just say "Looking forward to seeing you." This is an *elevator call* to lift someone up and make them feel good. Make these calls often!

- As you spend time with someone you learn about their needs, dreams and challenges. When you read something that relates to them, clip it, then write a note, e-mail or call. Make people feel special.
- Remember the Golden Rule, "Do unto others, as you would have them do unto you." It is essential to your success. You are responsible to keep your promises and be on time.
- Beyond the Golden Rule is the *Platinum Rule,* "Do unto others as they want to be done unto." The Golden Rule works in all situations, even with people you do not know. The Platinum Rule, named by Tony Alesandra, can be even more effective with people that you do know.
- When you meet someone to provide support, make sure you know their current status, and any recent numbers, without having to ask. Make it personal.
- Never forget you're in charge of your life. Make good choices. We always find time to do what we really *want-to-do,* so make connecting, sharing, and recruiting a *want-to-do.* There is nothing you can do that has a higher ROI – Return on Investment. Try it for 2 months and see.
- We've written a lot about one-on-one appointments. In personal or business situations we are often talking to more than one person. If this is the case, be sure to find a way to include them in the conversation. Try saying, "What do you think?" or "How does this sound to you?" It's a good way to be considerate and engage the other person who may be interested as well.
- Create involved listeners by having people participate in structuring the conversation. Ask simple questions like, "Is this a good time to _____? Would you be interested in hearing _____? If I could show you how to _____ (be/do/have something they want) is it a good time?"

Appreciate What You Have in Direct Sales!

You are a rare exception if you do not have to earn a living to pay the rent and survive. You are also an exception if you can do this without having to get up to go to work at hours somebody else has set and are able to take time off without permission.

To become financially free you need to decide if you are willing to give up some things in the short-term to get to where you want to be. Is it important to you to watch TV every night or sit on a patio relaxing all weekend? Success in business comes from making good choices and investing enough time to get results. If you would like to have the time and money to do what you want, when you want, then you must focus on recruiting and building people. Create your plan, with a timeline, and act on it. Take the right actions every day and you can achieve everything your heart desires.

Can you even imagine the new friendships you're going to make? You'll be surrounded by people who, like you, want to build a better life. These people are likely to become your friends for life. You may go on trips with them to exotic places you've only dreamed about. You may create joyful memories of overcoming challenges and create amazing success stories together. Imagine great things and make them real!

You are connected to people who, like you, have a common mission to support other people by sharing what they know. You all support your personal growth by building others. There is great joy in sharing financial rewards and ideas that change and enrich lives.

If you never talked to a stranger, you might not be in the position you are in today to recruit and help other people. You are changing your life for the better and others lives too! You deserve applause!

You are living in a world now where there are no strangers, just new friends to meet - whom you can help by sharing the opportunity and the good times you've discovered.

RECRUIT!

It may never have occurred to you that you are extraordinary! But you are, you should know it and you should be proud. We're living in a time when we are surrounded with more takers than givers. You are a giver and that should be celebrated.

Every day we see people who have settled for less than they were meant to have. We all know people who live and act like victims and dig themselves into emotional and psychological holes then they struggle to get out of them. Not you! For some reason you reached out to an industry where you can be in charge of your life, your time, your money and your success.

Invest your time, and money to develop your natural skills for helping and sharing. Be strong and determined, and know the sacrifices you make now to build a business will pay off in extraordinary ways that you might not even be able to imagine.

Review this list of the things available to you. These gifts are yours for the taking, for your benefit, and for those you love and care about.

- You have extra income anytime you want it
- You have a way to get out of debt by doing good things
- You make money by caring and sharing
- You spend time with people that share your interests
- You choose your co-workers
- You live in a world rich with friendships – old and new
- You work with people that share your mission
- You're committed to helping people learn and grow
- You set a good example and are a role model for others
- You are in charge of your life and your future

So What's Next?

Ideas are a lot like food. If you are hungry, you want more. Then when you get more, often you get too much. When you have too much, you're uncomfortable and you tend to make all kinds of resolutions. It's time for a diet of thought. Feed yourself what you need to succeed.

You are so much luckier than most people. Whether you are working your business full time, as a part-time source of extra income, or an investment in time now for what will someday become your career, we know you are serious or you wouldn't have read this far.

Review your goals

This is a good time to review your goals or to set some new ones. If you want to have meaningful goals, make them measurable (with numbers), specific (with a timeframe to accomplish them), realistic (things you believe you can achieve) and challenging (stretch and give consistent effort).

- Make sure you have your objectives, weekly and monthly goals in writing, and keep them where you can see them.
- Share them with someone you trust, such as your Leader, and ask them to hold you accountable.
- Commit to consistent efforts to get results.
- Always remember to celebrate your accomplishments and then set new goals.

This book has given you many things to sit and ThinkAbout, plus many action steps to take to build your personal skills and your team's skills, by talking, writing, self-evaluating, analyzing, role playing, and group discussions.

If you have worked through, rather than just read through it, you should be feeling pretty good about connecting with people, sharing your business opportunity to build your team, and stepping up to a Leadership role in your company. If you promoted yourself since you picked up the book, congratulations!

This book can't make you a Leader or build your team, only you can do that. It's a springboard to success for you and all of the people you choose to share these techniques and this information with as you grow into Leadership. Becoming a Leader takes daily action and a daily focus on sharing your business opportunity.

Make connections

Connect with new people every day. Be prepared to do business every time you leave your house, both physically (by having your marketing materials, product samples, and business cards with you) and more importantly, mentally and emotionally. Have your head in the sharing game. Believe that you offer a worthwhile opportunity to make money and for people to take charge of their destiny, to create a life and lifestyle of their dreams, by working alongside of you in your company.

When new people join your team, personally commit to show them how to succeed, and match their efforts to grow. You are responsible to give them the tools they need and to show the way. They are responsible to do the work necessary to achieve their own success at the level they choose.

Challenge yourself to connect with people and share your information, and also to conclude these conversations by asking them to choose one of three things:

1. To join you as a business builder and make money
2. To introduce you to their friends and family and save money
3. To buy the great product that you offer and experience the excellent service you provide along with the rewards of being a customer of your company

As you use the ideas in this book to share and recruit consistently, you are building your growing team. You are learning to work with people to develop their skills to achieve their personal and financial dreams. You are becoming a Leader of people, a truly honorable position because you will lead from the heart, using your head and sharing your skills. You will recognize your team and make them feel valued and valuable.

I remember having a plaque on my home office wall when I was a young Leader myself. It said, "Leaders are not born, they are made." ThinkAbout it! Leadership skills develop over time by working with a lot of different people. Leaders keep learning and growing and bringing more people along as they climb the ladder to success. Always reach up with one hand for the next rung on the ladder, while you reach back with the other hand to pull someone up with you.

Apply what you have learned

Take my challenge to apply what you have learned here. Keep this book close at hand and refer to it often as you develop the people on your team. Promise yourself that you'll keep growing, learning and sharing. These key actions create your personal cycle of success.

Long term growth and increased income takes consistent effort over time to create a strong foundation. It requires sharing, teaching, training, coaching, and mentoring people, many people. Become excellent at what you do. Strive to bring out the best in everyone you meet. Develop an eye for human potential and earnestly work to develop it for the success of others.

Enjoy the fruits of your efforts together with your team. Create shared memories and celebrations, aim high, keep dreaming and keep achieving! Enjoy the rewards of your success. You earned and you deserve it!

Activator Topic Reference

Sharing - *Create Security and Team Success* 13

Helping- *Changing People's lives* 15

Growing - *Creating person growth by nurturing others* 17

Stretching- *Strengthen your recruiting muscles* 19

Planning- *Organizing for Success* 21

Why People Don't Recruit - *Eliminate excuses* 27

Embarrassed? - *Learning to share in social settings* 29

Not Everyone Likes Selling - *Start generating curiosity* 31

Is the Picture Too Big? - *Getting a decision to start* 33

Who Do You Know? - *Connecting with more people* 41

Overlooking Obvious Prospects - *We all tune-out sometimes* 45

Think about Products and Services - *Offering everyone opportunities* 47

Utilize the Power of the Phone - *Connecting near and far* 49

Walk Through the Door - *Prepare to promote yourself* 53

Zero-in When You Have a Cue - *Filling others needs* 55

Are You a Rescuer? - *Enhancing listening skills* 59

To Be Serious, Be Serious - *Recommendations for success* 97

Don't Scare the New Recruits - *Plenty of people for everyone* 103

Some Things are Easy - *Developing the recruiting habit* 115

Farmer's Story - *Building in your own backyard* 123

Thank you from Ro

For all who have influenced my life and career.

Sandi & Roger Mullins, Cora Fischer, Rosemarie Fagan, Miriam Loizzo, Diana & Bob Ruffolo, Susie Lite, Betti Wasek, Nancy Medin, Susan Pestine, Judy & Bob Shales, Mary Ciombar, Pam & Paul Miller, Pam Davis, Ann & Kevin Raulston, Brenda Stefanowski, Julie Mucha, Patricia Brose, Rosemary Redmond, Barbara Keeney, Julie Soudek, Karen Starich, Jeanette Zachs, Jean Coltrain, Maria Triantos, Risa Roe, Melinda Jensen, Ann Nelson, Lorene Bohn, Lisa Teubel, Riki McManus, Jim Caldwell, Craig Parkhurst, Linda Herrick, Julia Carrol, Barbara Jack, Cindy Juncaj, Mark Bosworth, Mikki Lessard, Amy Mullen, Marsha Mitchell, Joy Grimm, Bobbi Pennel, PK Rugh, Carlene Schrank, Deidre Taylor, Sheryl Hughey, Renee Stovall-White, Jackie Geisinger, Dyan Lucero, Judi Brewster, Connie Tang, Dorothy Olson, Bonnie Strigenz, Gina O'Neill, Susan Hall, Darleen Moss, Cherie Daugherty, Tom & Carol Judson, Pamela Randisi, Molly Klipp, Karen McCarter, Bob & Ann Marie Roche, Dana Davin, Nancy Salverino, Stephanie Jarvis, Marguerite Bencivenga, Mary Kaskie, Cate Brusenbach, Dorothy Hall, Sharon Baldauf Gitzen, Sarah Baldauf, Jerry & Joan Baldauf, Greg & Audrey Baldauf, Cathy Welsch Lichter, Emily Parmalee, Renee Carlson, Steve Klopfer, Mary & Lee Tamraz, Susan Becker-Doroshow, Eunice Sullivan, Mary Maragos, Peggy Kasimatis, Cindy Riley, Judy Pitte, Beverly Jambois, Joyce Erickson, Rose Mifflin, Maggie Mongan, Bill & Irene Baldauf, Brenda Dahl, Marge Jacobson, Blake Cahoon, Linda San Filippo, Judy Walthers, Donna Baldauf Kemp, Christine Sonnen, Robb, Robbie & Ricky Shales, George & Sally Baldauf…

An extra special thank you to these smart women for their assistance with this book - Julie Mucha, Brenda Dahl, Linda San Filippo & Lisa Teubel.

Thank you from G. Sherle

There aren't enough words to say THANKS.

Kathy & Michael Richer, Steve & Peggy Adams, Todd & Barbara Lowe, Candy Woods Lindley, Barbara Barker, Penny Pace, Neil Offen, John Kiple, Madeline Johnson, Doris Christopher, Sarah Moseley, Lewis Rasmussen, Curt Carlson, Frank Vander Sloot, Buckminster Fuller, Alice Westbrook Barnes, Jerry Vinopal, Nona Pione, J C Penny, Robb Shales, Phil Humbert Ph.D., Cleo Hovel, Theresa Soloma, Howard Eyrich, Ph.D., Dr. Bill Rose, Ph.D., Paul Meihl Ph.D., Gary Cox Pastor, Sister Dolorice, Debra Poneman, Frank Piper...

There are many others...You are loved and appreciated!

Ordering RECRUIT!

Order extra copies of RECRUIT! as gifts, team incentives, for meetings, workshops, and to loan out to new recruits. Please share RECRUIT! with your friends and co-workers!

Contact us for quantity discounts on 12, 24, or 48 copies.
www.imaginativeconsulting.com/our-new-book

Planning an Event?

Ro Shales delivers custom presentations for your team or company.
With broad experience in a wide variety of Direct Selling companies, Ro understands both the field, and management side of the industry.
And as a long-time volunteer, she also relates to the challenges of non-profit recruiting.

"Ro Shales is one of the best. She always gives an excellent presentation. Ro has a natural ability to connect to 10 or 10,000 and make her audience members feel she is talking directly to them. Everything she does is personalized and her love of sharing shines through."
~ Grandma Sherle

About the Authors

Roseann Shales

Roseann "Ro" Shales was introduced to Direct Sales right out of college when she decided to become a Tupperware Consultant and try six home parties. She stayed for 18 years, building a sales team that grew to average over $1 million a year in sales and 35 Leader promotions a year when the average party was $200 and the average customer order was $22. She and her Leader team recruited and trained thousands of people.

She went on to work corporately for several well-known companies on their management teams, including Weekenders USA, PartyLight, JAFRA Cosmetics Int'l and Aloette Cosmetics. She has also started companies from scratch and turned others around. Her company, Imaginative Consulting, "IC", indicates her approach to challenges, "I see…and what if…? Expect more books and innovative services from "IC" during 2012.

Ro has built a reputation as a "Connector," bringing people and ideas together. Her passions are creating a recruiting culture and empowering people to become their best selves. Ro lives in Wisconsin with her husband Robb and their college age sons, Robbie and Ricky and the family dog Rosie.

You can connect with her at ro@roshales.com

G. Sherle Maguire Adams

Sherle Maguire Adams, aka "Grandma Sherle" is well known as a communication guru. Early in her career, she starred in the ad agency world in new product development, marketing, and award winning sales promotion. During her "working years" she created a list of "firsts" over 8 pages long. She's written 28 books and programs. Her mantra is, "When in doubt-reach out!"

You may have heard Sherle speak at a national convention, or at numerous leadership and motivational workshops. She has keynoted for numerous companies and associations including, National Sales Executives, and for her favorite, the Direct Selling Association (DSA) annual meeting and workshops. Neil Offen, former President of the DSA, referred to her as a "legend".

Sherle has appeared many times on TV and Radio in the USA and Canada talking about having a YOB (Your Own Business) vs. having a JOB and her favorite subject revolving around her belief that we all are "only words apart."

Her resume includes working with many Generals: General Motors, General Mills, General Foods, General Electric and General Eisenhower, plus US Gypsum, US Steel and the US Government.

Ro and Sherle are working on several other writing projects. At 91 years young, Sherle has a goal to become the "Grandma Moses of Publishing." She resides in Alabama with her loving husband John. Contact her at SherleAdams@bellsouth.net

In case you're wondering

Ro and Grandma Sherle met when Sherle was being flown around the country in a private jet by Tupperware to speak at six summer Jubilees, their annual conference. After Sherle spoke on stage, Ro approached her to tell her she enjoyed her presentation and also asked Sherle to have a Tupperware party. It turned out they both lived in the suburbs of Chicago, and Sherle said *Yes*. She hosted a successful fundraiser. They've been connected ever since.

A booklet was created for Tupperware with some of Sherle's ideas from those events. Ro used them in her early years in Direct Sales to enhance her recruiting skills and to build her own successful sales team.

Visit www.imaginativeconsulting.com

for your FREE Leader Guide to compliment this book.

While you're there please take a moment to complete the RECRUIT! Feedback Survey.

We want to know how RECRUIT! helps you!
Share your ideas and you may be included in the next edition.

Join our mailing list! Visit the site often for business building tips, training ideas, and marketing information.